THE RED MARKET

THE
RED MARKET

On the Trail of the World's Organ
Brokers, Bone Thieves, Blood Farmers,
and Child Traffickers

SCOTT CARNEY

WILLIAM MORROW
An Imprint of HarperCollins *Publishers*

Portions of this book previously appeared, in slightly different form, in the following publications: chapter 2, "The Bone Factory," in *Wired*, December 2007; chapter 3, "Kidney Prospecting," on Wired.com, July 2007; chapter 4, "Meet the Parents," in *Mother Jones*, March/April 2009; chapter 5, "Immaculate Conception," in *Fast Company*, September 2010; chapter 6, "Cash on Delivery," in *Mother Jones*, March/April 2010; chapter 8, "The Clinical Labor of Guinea Pigs," on Nerve.com; chapter 10, "Black Gold," in *Mother Jones*, March/April 2010.

Library of Congress Cataloging-in-Publication Data has been applied for.

ISBN 978-0-06-193646-3

15   OV/RRD   10 9 8 7 6 5

For my parents,
Linda Haas Carney
and
Wilfred Ignatius Carney Jr.

If blood as a living human tissue is increasingly bought and sold as an article of commerce and profit accrues from such transactions then it follows that the laws of commerce must, in the end, prevail.

—*Richard Titmuss,* THE GIFT RELATIONSHIP

In other parts of India, people say that they are going to Malaysia or the United States with a glimmer of hope in their eyes. In Tsunami Nagar people speak that way about selling their kidneys.

—*Maria Selvam, activist, India*

CONTENTS

PREFACE   DEAD END   xi

INTRODUCTION   MAN VS. MEAT   1
ONE   BODY ALCHEMY   21
TWO   THE BONE FACTORY   39
THREE   KIDNEY PROSPECTING   61
FOUR   MEET THE PARENTS   91
FIVE   IMMACULATE CONCEPTION   111
SIX   CASH ON DELIVERY   135
SEVEN   BLOOD MONEY   153
EIGHT   CLINICAL LABOR OF GUINEA PIGS   175
NINE   IMMORTAL PROMISES   197
TEN   BLACK GOLD   221
AFTERWORD   ODE TO LORETTA HARDESTY   231

ACKNOWLEDGMENTS   239
BIBLIOGRAPHY   243
INDEX   247

A bag of tibias recovered on the Indo-Bhutanese border town of Jaigaon. The evidence locker had more than one hundred skulls that had been pillaged from graves—most likely Muslim graveyards in Varanasi. I came here expecting to find anatomy specimens destined for US medical programs, but learned that these materials would be turned into flutes and sold to Tibetan Buddhists inside Bhutan.

DEAD END

THE SUBINSPECTOR WORKS the last breath out of a waning cigarette and flicks it out the window. The butt lands on foreign soil. The squat concrete police station that he presides over hugs the border so tightly that simply walking across the room might put him in another country's jurisdiction. Responsible for overseeing contraband flowing between the world's largest democracy and its last absolute monarchy, the officer spends his time reading the newspapers and calculating the surreal distance between himself and Delhi. He searches in his shirt pocket for another smoke, but the pack is empty. Frowning, he looks across the desk and ponders my request.

"So you want to see the skeletons."

I'm not sure if it is a question or a statement. I shift my weight on the wooden stool; it creaks as I pull it forward. I nod.

For two weeks I've been combing the state of West Bengal on an assignment to investigate reports of so-called bone factories.

For more than a century graves have turned up empty across the Indian countryside, the bodies sold abroad as anatomical skeletons. Until recently the trade was so extensive that just about every classroom skeleton in America must have come from India. In 1985 the Indian government banned exports of human materials, and many bone dealers were forced out of business. A few still existed though, driven underground—and like other businesses on the red market, they were thriving.

I've made my way to the Indo-Bhutanese border to document the supply chain of one particularly odious anatomist who is said to still have connections with Western companies. But as profitable as the business might be, the places where the bones actually get processed aren't much to look at. The elusive bone factories are really just small tarp lean-tos posted on the banks of rivers. Here endless streams of cadavers get reduced to their most basic parts. Bone dealers employ grave robbers and self-trained anatomists to strip the flesh from the bodies, polish what is left to a chalk-white patina, and package them for shipping. The gruesome business is not popular with locals and police, so the dealers work out of sight. It had taken me three full weeks to find a lead.

My break came when a newspaper ran a short story about a police outpost that had seized a cache of skulls and bones in a lucky bust. I trekked out to the Jaigaon crossing, a border town that sees thousands of transients a day but isn't famous for hospitality.

"So you want to see the skulls." The officer smirks. "That won't be a problem."

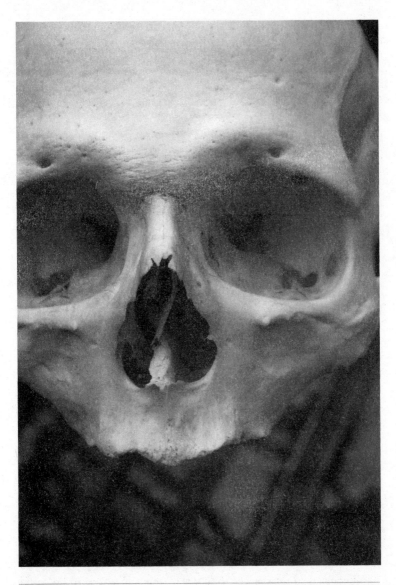

This human skull was part of a cache of similar material recovered by police outside Kolkata, India. The teeth have fallen out, making this specimen far less valuable than a more intact skull. It smelled faintly of fried chicken.

He gets up from his desk and gestures for me to follow him to an open window; its dirt-smeared pane of glass overlooks the Indian side of the border. He points at a squat concrete building next door. "They set up right there. Three rooms full of bones." The traders didn't have to deal with the border security; they could throw the bags of contraband over the walls into the neighboring country. Still, it was a bad plan to set up next to a police station.

"To tell you the truth," he says, "this isn't much of a problem. We were worried that these might have been murder victims. I don't think that there is any specific law against robbing graves in this country. They will probably walk free." Even charging them with theft is a problem since the bones' original owners are now all dead.

After the arrest, the police logged the bones in as evidence just in case a court ever decides to hear the charges. The cop's assistant takes me to a stained jail cell that doubles as an interrogation room and evidence locker. The man pulls out a half dozen old cement bags made of woven nylon. He drops one on the floor, and the dry bones inside clatter. He fumbles with the knot and pulls back a layer of clear plastic.

The first is full of leg bones. They smell of earth. The clots of dirt clinging to them tell me that they have been sitting in the ground for a long time. A few of the tibias have saw marks where the workers cut off the knobby ends into what looks like a mouthpiece for a flute. The coolie yanks on a brown hemp string that ties the second bag shut and reveals that it is full of skulls. Each skull had been sawed into pieces so that the area below the crown could be removed and discarded; all that is left are about one hundred brainpans.

I frown as I look over the supply. These are not the skulls that I am looking for. They're too old and too processed. A good anatomical skeleton has to be prepared quickly, and the bones systematically cleaned to be useful. Once they've been in the ground for too long there's no chance that an aspiring doctor would find them useful for study. Besides, what doctor isn't going to want to see the rest of the skeleton? It dawns on me that I've found the wrong damn bone traders. The people who stole these had a different business plan. They're not marketing to doctors, they're marketing to monks.

Certain sects of Bhutanese Buddhism are unique in that they teach that the only way to understand mortality is to spend time contemplating dead bodies up close. As such, almost every family and earnest Buddhist practitioner needs carefully prepared ritual instruments crafted out of human bones. Most commonly, this means flutes carved from tibias, and prayer bowls cut from the crowns of skulls, hence the bags full of them.

I'm used to dead ends, and yet I'm still surprised. I hadn't expected that there would be multiple ways to sell a stolen skeleton. I snap a few photos and thank the cops for their time. I'd wasted the day and a half that it took to get here.

My driver fires up the engine and peels out of the police station driveway, kicking up a cloud of brown dust behind us. I prepare myself for another interminable journey of bumpy roads and near-head-on collisions as we play chicken with oncoming traffic. In the levity that comes with imminent mortality, I think about how unlikely it is to have two sets of bone thieves competing for bodies in rural India. Are markets for body parts something that exist only on the fringes of international commerce? How many ways can there be to sell a human body?

If in this remote corner of the planet people are fighting over bodies and exporting the remains of dead people, then it figures that other people are probably profiting on bodies in other parts of the world, too. Maybe every one of our human parts—from bones, ligaments, corneas, hearts, blood to whole human beings—trades hands every day.

I don't know it yet, but this is just the beginning of my investigation into the world's red markets. I will travel across India, Europe, Africa, and the United States finding industries—both legal and illegal—that traffic in the buying and selling of human body parts. The body bazaar is bigger than I ever could have imagined.

THE RED MARKET

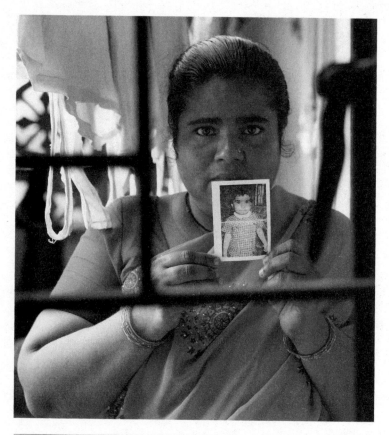

Fatima has been searching for her daughter Zabeen for almost nine years. The cost of investigating the kidnapping has bankrupted their family, and they now live in a small concrete hutment on top of a building in Washermanpet, Chennai, India. Court records showed that Zabeen had been sent to Australia. Activists have been working to arrange a reunion for several years.

INTRODUCTION
MAN VS. MEAT

I WEIGH JUST a little under two hundred pounds, have brown hair, blue eyes, and a full set of teeth. As far as I know, my thyroid gland pumps the right hormones into the twelve pints of blood that circulate in my arteries and veins. At six feet two inches, I have long femurs and tibias with solid connective tissue. Both of my kidneys function properly, and my heart runs at a steady clip of eighty-seven beats per minute. All in, I figure I'm worth about $250,000.

My blood separates neatly into plasma, red blood cells, platelets, and clotting factor and would save the life of someone on an operating table or stem the uncontrolled spilling of a hemophiliac's blood. The ligaments that keep me together can be scraped from my bones and implanted in the wounded knee of an Olympian athlete. The hair on my head could be made into a wig, or reduced to amino acids and sold as a leavening agent for baked goods. My skeleton would make a striking addition to any biology classroom. My major organs—heart, liver, and kidneys—could go on to prolong the lives of people whose organs have failed, and my corneas could be sliced off to restore sight to the blind. Even after death a determined pathologist could harvest my sperm and use it to help a woman conceive. The woman's baby would have a value of its own.

Since I'm an American, my flesh sells at a premium; if I had been born in China, I would be worth much, much less. The doctors and brokers, no matter the country, who would move the pieces of my body through the markets stand to make a considerable sum—much more than I could as a seller—for their services. It turns out that the global laws of supply and demand are as fixed in organ markets as they are for shoes and electronics.

In the same way that a mechanic can swap out worn car parts for new ones and oil creaky joints to get an engine running again, a surgeon can prolong someone's life by trading broken pieces for newer ones. Every year the technology barriers get lower and the process cheaper. But there's no scrap heap for quality used human parts. Attempts to create artificial hearts, kidneys, and blood pale in comparison to the real thing. The human body is just too complex. At the moment the body can't be replicated in a factory or lab. Which means the only way we can meet the demand for body parts is to find sources of raw materials in the population of living and recently deceased people.

We need great volumes of human material to supply medical schools with cadavers so that future doctors have a solid understanding of human anatomy. Adoption agencies send thousands of children from the third world to the first to fill the gaps in the American family unit. Pharmaceutical companies need live people to test the next generation of superdrugs, and the beauty industry processes millions of pounds of human hair every year to quench a ceaseless demand for new hairstyles. Forget the days of grass-skirt-wearing cannibals on tropical islands, our appetite for human flesh is higher now than at any other time in history.

There is a strange alchemy that happens when we decide that a human body can be swapped on the open market. Most people instinctively know that what makes humans special is more than just our physical presence—from the electrons and quarks that give us mass to the complex biological structures that sustain our every breath; there is also a sense of presence, which only accompanies life. For the purpose of this book and to make sense of it as I write, I give the human body the benefit of a soul.* Losing that soul transforms a body into a jumble of matter.

Though we like to think that our bodies are sacred and above the hardscrabble logic of the market, the sale of human parts is booming. Several billion dollars' worth of humanity changes hands every year. With almost six billion people in the world the supply is significant. There are just slightly fewer than six billion spare kidneys (or twelve billion if you are absolutely merciless) and almost sixty billion liters of blood in the global supply. There are enough corneas to fill a soccer stadium. The only thing stopping businesses from grabbing the potential profits are the rights to mine the resources.

---

* There is a long and convoluted philosophical and theological tradition on the existence or lack of existence of a soul that I am not qualified to engage in. The concept of a soul is useful to parse out the difference between the specialness of animated humans and the simple physical matter that makes us up. There is a clear difference between the living and dead, and that specialness—whatever it may be—is the rock I've built this book upon.

Take, for instance, the market for adopted children. At the moment a family decides they want to bring in a needy child from a foreign country, they only have an abstract idea about that child's identity. In their search for the perfect baby they refine their expectations based on the available baby market. They troll through online menus issued by international adoption agencies, read newspaper articles about desperate children in orphanages, and make difficult decisions about what particular set of characteristics will trigger the adoption.

Sure, at some point the child will be a member of the family, but to actually obtain one they have to engage with an often shady supply chain of middlemen and corruptible government officials, many of whom see children as little more than bodies. It is only after they have brought the child into their home that the child transforms from an abstraction into someone real.

It doesn't matter what our moral position is on the subject, bodies are unquestionably commodities. And yet they are uncomfortable ones. As a product, bodies aren't assembled new in factories filled with sterile suited workers; rather they are harvested like used cars at scrap markets. Before you can write a check and pick up human tissue, someone needs to transform it from a tiny piece of humanity into something with a market value. Unlike scrap, the price of a human body isn't measured only in dollars. It is measured in blood, and in the ineffable value of lives both saved and lost. When we buy a body part, we take on the liabilities for where it came from both ethically and in terms of the previous owner's biological and genetic history. It's a transaction that never really ends.

·   ·   ·   ·

LAW AND ECONOMICS RECOGNIZE three types of markets: white, gray, and black. Black markets trade in illegal goods and services like guns and drug running while bootleg DVDs and nontaxed income fall into legal gray areas. White markets are the territory of everything legal and aboveboard—from the groceries that are purchased at a corner bodega to the income taxes that are dutifully filed every year. All three of these markets have two common features: the things being traded have real-world values that can be easily reduced to dollars and cents, and the transactions end the minute money changes hands. Markets in flesh are different because their customers owe their lives and family relationships to the supply chain.

Welcome to the red market.

Red markets are the product of contradictions that arise when social taboos surrounding the human body collide with the individual urge to live a long, happy life. If commodity markets can be figured with algebra, red markets require calculus. Every equation holds both a zero and infinity. Red markets occur on the cusp of major life-changing events for either the supplier or the buyer. Whether the buyer acknowledges it or not, flesh creates a lifelong debt to the person who supplied it.

Because of this bond and because we tend to reject the language of commercialism when dealing with bodies, all red markets also share a curious language of altruism throughout the transaction. Kidneys, blood, and human eggs are "donated," not sold. Adoptive parents take in needy children, they're not adding to the size of their own family.

And yet, despite these links, the dollar prices for human bodies and body parts are well established and the supply is, thanks in part to burgeoning populations in impoverished parts of the world, nearly limitless.

In Egypt, India, Pakistan, and the Philippines, entire villages sell organs, rent wombs, and sign away rights to their bodies after death—not only under duress, but also in mutually agreeable trans- actions. Middlemen who deal in human parts—often hospitals and government institutions, but sometimes the most unscrupulous criminals—buy for the lowest possible price while assuring buyers that the parts come from ethical sources. Though procurement is sometimes abhorrent, the final sale is often legal and usually sanc- tioned by the implicit moral dimension of saving human lives. The crimes are covered up in a veil of altruistic ideals.

Unlike any other transaction we are likely to make in our lives, buying on the red market makes us indebted to all of the links between the source of parts and the final outcome. There are few other transactions that immediately raise ethical red flags as buying parts of other people. The question of what makes an "ethical source" is one that every potential beneficiary of the red market needs to take seriously.

If we need our body to live, then how can any part of it pos- sibly be spared? In a case of live organ donation, how can a sick person become entitled to the organs of a healthy person? What criteria have to be met to move a child from the third world to the first? Inevitably red markets have the nasty social side effect of moving flesh upward—never downward—through social classes. Even without a criminal element, unrestricted free markets act like vampires, sapping the health and strength from ghettos of poor donors and funneling their parts to the wealthy.

Proponents of unrestricted red markets often suggest that

people who willingly sell their tissue benefit from the transaction. The money will supposedly pull them up from the depths of poverty into a higher social station. After all, shouldn't we all be able to make decisions about what happens to our own bodies? The logic, presumably, is that human tissue is a last-ditch social safety net, and when sold can act as a lifeline to lift a person out of a desperate situation. The reality is that people who sell bodies and body parts rarely see their lives improved. Sociologists have long known that this is a fantasy.* There are no long-term benefits to selling parts of your body, only risks.

There is only one situation where someone's social station can rise at the same speed as the price of a body part. And it only happens when the whole body is sold all at once: when babies enter the international adoption market.

With millions of orphans in the world, adoption alleviates, on the face of it, an important social problem. Children invariably move from precarious positions on the edges of society into financially stable, caring homes. But like any other market, adoptions are subject to the pressures of scarcity. The West, which accounts for the most international adoptions, demands lighter-skin babies, leaving orphanages racially skewed. Domestically, orphanages become an unfortunate lens into racial politics in America. White

---

* There is a wealth of academic literature on the social side effects of selling kidneys. While there are many active proponents of organ markets, those articles are most often written by economists and transplant surgeons. For some representative examples of studies see Lawrence Cohen's "Where It Hurts," which appeared in a 1999 issue of *Dædalus*. Or the straightforwardly name named article "Economic and Health Consequences of Selling a Kidney in India" by Madhav Goyal et al., in the October 2002 issue of *JAMA*. Also see the bibliography of this book.

orphans tend to get adopted almost immediately by eager parents, while black orphans often grow up in the foster care system.

The problem is worse abroad, where the primary criterion isn't the ethnicity, but rather the health of the child. In India, China, Samoa, Zambia, Guatemala, Romania, and Korea, poorly resourced orphanages are known to stunt child development. As terrible as it may sound, in these places—and across much of the third world—the business model of adoption most closely resembles the market for bananas. If either a child or a fruit spends too much time in storage, it isn't worth much on the market. Only children who have had short stints inside the institutions have a chance of finding a home, and orphanages often reap lucrative adoption fees for every international adoption. While children do move upward in social standing through adoptions, the discrepancy between storage and a bill of sale means that adoption agencies need either a high turnover rate or an innovative way to acquire children on short notice. The problem has both legal and illegal solutions.

UNTIL THE 1970S THE world experimented with open commerce in body parts. The battles over whether flesh should be legal or illegal were fought first, and most conclusively, over blood. In 1901 the Viennese scientist Karl Landsteiner discovered that there were four discrete blood types and helped usher in the era of safe blood transfusions. Prior to that, getting a blood transfusion was like playing Russian roulette. You might live, or you might die painfully, on the operating table, while baffled surgeons scratched their heads as the incompatible blood types coagulated. Landsteiner's discovery was just in time for World War I, when hundreds of thousands of direct person-to-person transfusions helped keep soldiers alive on the battlefield. By World War II, blood banks had the storage capacity to make blood an essential weapon of war that kept soldiers alive to fight another day. Blood-collecting clinics met the surging demand by offering cash to anyone willing to give up a pint. The immediate benefit of readily available blood meant that doctors could perform more extensive surgeries than they had before. Blood loss was no longer an impediment to surgery. The development led to advances across the field of medicine.

It also meant that collection centers grew into big businesses. By 1956 clinics in the United States were paying for more than five million pints annually. Ten years later reserves tipped six million pints. Blood-collection shops sprang up in skid-row shantytowns of every major city. They became as commonplace as check-cashing stores and pawnshops are today in the same areas. In India, national unions negotiated blood rates with the government, and soon professional donors plied their trade in every major city on the Indian subcontinent.

The blood business was saving lives, and few people troubled with the ethics of the supply chain. It took until 1970 for a British social anthropologist named Richard Titmuss to express his concern that body markets were creating unequal access to medical advancement. Titmuss was influenced by his own country's ethical stance on the issue. England invented blood drives during World War II and millions of people donated to help the war effort without expecting to be paid. Even after the war, hospitals almost never paid for blood; rather, British people saw it as their patriotic duty to give. In his book *The Gift Relationship,* Titmuss compared the commercial system in the United States to the altruistic one in England and made two main arguments.

First he showed that buying blood increased incidents of hepatitis in the blood supply and drove hospitals and blood banks to rely on increasingly coercive measures to increase stocks in human blood. Bought blood was dangerous. It was also exploitative. Commercial collection led the state to seek the cheapest possible sources. They started turning to prisoners to donate blood: a situation that he likened to a modern-era version of slavery. The same sort of exploitation, he said, had the potential to spring up in any other market in human tissue.

Second, Titmuss argued that the only way to solve the problem would be to create a system based exclusively on altruistic donation. He believed that blood-donation systems could do more than save lives and create profits for hospitals. He thought they could build communities, too. He wrote: "those who give as members of society to strangers will themselves (or their families) eventually benefit as members of society."* For Titmuss, bodies and body parts should only be exchanged as gifts. Think of it as blood socialism.

Remarkably, and despite massive opposition by the commercial blood lobby, people listened. The United States passed laws that made voluntary donation the norm. Paying for blood of any kind was now considered coercion and brought stiff penalties. (Though it should be noted that not all blood was created equal.

---

* Richard Titmuss, *The Gift Relationship* (London: George Allen & Unwin Ltd., 1970), 215.

They made an exception for blood plasma, which is easier for the body to regenerate; it continues to be a frequent source of side income for many people across the United States.) And the trend spread across all other markets in human tissue.

In 1984 on the floor of the US Senate, Al Gore famously proclaimed that "the body should not be a mere assemblage of spare parts" when he helped pass a national law that forbade payments for any type of human flesh. After invoking Titmuss in the halls of government, the Senate voted in favor of the National Organ Transplant Act and explicitly banned the sale of human organs and tissue. The world followed suit. Today, with just a few notable exceptions, it is illegal in every country to sell blood, buy a kidney, buy a child for adoption, or sell your skeleton in advance of death. Instead we have complex systems set up to give consent for voluntary harvesting. We donate our blood at blood banks, sign organ donation cards, and will our bodies to scientific institutions after we die. All for free. In theory, anyone who takes money in exchange for a body part could wind up in jail. The law is unambiguous: Buying bodies is bad.

Unfortunately the laws fell short of leeching profits from the body business. The system that Titmuss outlined and the rest of the world adopted has two fatal flaws. First, while individuals can't directly buy and sell bodies, doctors, nurses, ambulance drivers, lawyers, and administrators all can bill market rates for their services. You may not pay for a heart, but you definitely pay for a heart transplant. In effect, the cost of a heart migrates into the costs of services to acquire one. Hospitals and medical institutions increasingly turn profits on organ transplants; some even return revenues to shareholders. Everyone in the supply chain makes money except the actual donor. The ban on buying human body parts has allowed hospitals to acquire them essentially for free.

From a customer's perspective, the organ transplant business in the United States resembles Gillette's famous business model. Gillette charges next to nothing for the actual shaving handle, but charges an arm and a leg for the blades. Kidneys are no different. Sure you can't buy one, but installation costs for a certified used kidney can run close to half a million dollars.

As with any economic system, a free supply of raw materials is only an invitation to find new ways to utilize them. In the United States we generally do not question that demand for transplantable flesh is a fixed thing—something tied to an absolute number of emergency situations, like kidney failure. The existence of a five-year waiting list seems to be proof positive that the demand for organs far outstrips supply. But that may not be the case.

For forty years the United Network for Organ Sharing has consistently expanded the available pool of cadaver donors and yet has never caught up with demand for new organs. Instead the waiting list has only grown longer. As more organs become available, doctors add new, previously considered unqualified patients to the transplant list. Transplant techniques and patient outcomes are always improving as surgeons discover that an even wider number of people can be helped with donor material. The transplant list disguises the reality that there isn't a fixed demand for organs. The length of the list is a function of the overall supply of available organs. Demand is a function of supply. The good news is that many people's lives are being extended this way. However, the limitless potential for expansion means that instead of only looking at the potential beneficial use of organs, we also need to be critically aware of how large and coercive the system of collecting organs can become.

To use an analogy, there seems to be an almost limitless demand for oil products in the world. Innovations with petroleum energy have led to unheralded economic, technological, and social gains. Distances have shrunk with the use of cars, there is light at night and heat in the winter. However, this does not mean that drilling and burning those products into extinction is necessarily the best thing for humankind.

The second flaw in Titmuss's model is that he failed to account for basic standards of medical privacy. While authorities might be able to track down an individual donor in their records, they are sealed from any sort of public scrutiny. It is simply not possible for anyone outside the hospital to discover the identity of the blood donor whose sacrifice has saved a life in surgery. The blood is depersonalized, marked with a bar code and poured into hermetically sealed plastic bags. We buy units of blood, not parts of people. The prevailing medical logic is that to connect the dots between donor and receiver could compromise the entire system, maybe even stop people from donating their tissue in the first place.

The person who receives the blood doesn't feel indebted to an individual donor, but to the system of blood donation in general, and specifically to the doctor who provides the service. Someone who receives a kidney, whether from a living donor or from a cadaver, rarely knows the person who gave up the organ. Though anonymity is meant to protect the interests of the donor, it also obscures the supply chain. Recipients buy tissue without ever having to worry about how it was procured in the first place. This sort of privacy is the last bit of alchemy that transforms human flesh into a commodity.

Obscuring the source of raw materials for any market is almost always a bad idea. We would never allow an oil company to hide the locations of its oil rigs, or not to disclose its environmental policies. And when an oil rig fails and leaks millions of barrels of petroleum into the ocean, we demand accountability. Transparency is capitalism's most basic safety feature.

From the perspective of a criminal entrepreneur, the current system of tissue collection is a perfect storm for rampant and unmitigated exploitation. Donation-only policies make it illegal to pay for tissue, and while companies may invest heavily in transplant infrastructure in the same way an oil company invests in a rig, the actual price of the raw materials is often nearly zero. Meanwhile the rhetoric around privacy obscures the path that bodies and body parts take to the market. Anonymity means that organ buyers can purchase human flesh without worrying about where it comes from. Nobody is going to ask any questions. The structure of donations neatly takes care of any objections by masking the supply behind a curtain of ethics. The one-two punch of anonymity and donation means that profit-taking middlemen control the entire supply chain, and buying an organ is as easy as writing a check.

In part, this book is an investigation of what has gone wrong with the current system of tissue harvesting and body procuring. Red markets are now larger, more pervasive, and more profitable than at any other time in history. In the forty years since Titmuss published his book, globalization has made the speed and complexity of these markets bewildering. This is not a wholesale indictment or embrace of commercialization. We live within the red market. It is not something that will simply vanish if we reject the idea that there is an economy built around human tissue. Whether we like it or not, the human body will be bought and sold both covertly and openly in the world's most respected institutions. The only question is how.

By and large, I have not focused on the millions of red market transactions that go right every day. There is no doubt that without transplant technology, blood collection, and adoption programs there would be terrible human fallout. We don't need to follow the stories of people living happy lives because of something they bought on the red market. That is the story of tissue demand. It is far more important to understand how tissue makes it to the market than how it is used. This book is an exploration of the supply side of the economic equation. Without understanding supply we will never understand how quickly red markets can foster global criminal enterprises.

The collision of altruism and privacy undercuts the noble ideals that they were meant to protect. Every step along the red market supply chain helps transform humans into meat. The brokers who buy and sell bodies play the part of butchers who can see a living person as nothing more than the sum of their constituent parts.

HOW IT ALL STARTED

FROM 2006 TO 2009 I lived in Chennai, a booming coastal metropolis in southern India, just a few hundred miles north of Sri Lanka.

Prior to that I had spent several years in India studying folklore and language at university programs in the desert state of Rajasthan and near Dharamsala, where the Dalai Lama lives in exile. I knew that I wanted to spend more time in South Asia, but at first I wasn't sure that I was going to be a journalist. Fresh out of a graduate program in anthropology at the University of Wisconsin–Madison, I started my short-lived professional academic career teaching American students on a semester abroad in India.

I was in charge of twelve students as we traveled from Delhi to the holy city of Varanasi and the pilgrimage center of Bodh Gaya. At our last stop, one of my students died, leaving me and the other director in charge of returning her body to her family in the United States. I spent three days with her corpse staving off the inevitable process of decay. It was closer than I had ever been to a body before, and as she cooled and changed color, I confronted the physical nature of mortality.

More than anything else, her death taught me that every corpse has a stakeholder. As she made the transition from person to object, people seemed to come out of the woodwork to make demands on what was left of her material self. I spent much of that time negotiating with police, insurance companies, morticians, family members, and airlines to bring her home for burial.

Although I wasn't aware of it at the time, this was the beginning of my own understanding of the international market for human bodies. In a way, I was thrust into this subject by events largely beyond my control. The first section of this book deals directly with that event. Some readers may find it disturbing.

After she died I felt that I couldn't continue teaching. Eventually I started writing for *Wired* and *Mother Jones* magazines, as well as television channels and radio stations from my base in Chennai. My stories covered the business practices of kidney traders, skeleton thieves, blood pirates, and child kidnappers across South Asia. Later, I traveled through Europe and the United States cataloging the worst-case scenarios. In every case I was astonished to find that most people who buy a piece of a human have no idea what series of events had to happen to make that part available.

The idea of red markets being something special and apart from normal economic systems began with my investigations of bone traders and kidney thieves in India, but the concept encompasses more than just bodies that are being used for spare parts. The mix of misplaced altruism and privacy has serious implications for both the burial and adoption industries as well. When it comes to human bodies, the supply chain is always eerily the same.

As I began to contemplate putting all of my research into one book, I realized that there were more criminal red markets than I could ever hope to cover. I've left out landmark cases of morgue thefts across the United States, where funeral parlors sold the bodies they were entrusted to take care of to tissue-supply companies. The desecrated corpses were carved into surgical grafts and replacement tendons. I've ignored scandals around traveling museum exhibitions, where plastinated bodies of executed prisoners have been put on display. Likewise I've only briefly mentioned a report that more than one hundred thousand pituitary glands were stolen in England to produce human growth hormone. I make no mention of a recent report of Bolivian serial murderers who sold the fat of their victims to European beauty-supply companies that produce up-market facial creams. And every day the list grows. From the mid-1990s to 2000 the Israeli military harvested the corneas of Palestinian militants killed in combat. And deeper in history, at the turn of the nineteenth century a booming market for shrunken heads in Europe sparked tribal wars in South America. Providing an exhaustive account of every red market is beyond my abilities.

Instead, I hope this book offers a new way to look at markets in human bodies. By seeing the commonalities in these markets, we might come up with solutions to the problems in the tissue economy. Criminals operate in the darkest corners of our economic world. And yet they only exist because we let them. The brokers I have met have very few scruples about how they acquire human materials. They are driven by the simple capitalist axiom: Buy low and sell high. Brokers keep the supply chain away from prying eyes.

While there are often benefits to moving tissue and bodies between owners, middlemen open the door to dangerous abuses. The only way to get rid of them is to let the sun shine in and expose the entire supply chain from beginning to end. Every blood packet should be traceable to the original donor, every kidney come affixed with a name, every surrogate womb findable, and every adoption open. Each chapter tackles a different red market for human materials. Each is an exploration into the most salient, profitable, or disturbing scenarios I could find; together, they give a bird's-eye view of red markets across the world.

At present, the power to track human materials through supply chains tentatively rests in the hands of administrative agencies. By and large, these groups are underfunded and often work hand in glove with the hospitals and brokers they are meant to oversee. International transactions often have no oversight at all. Their failures are well documented in every market I cover in this book. Instead of blindly trusting them to safely manage the process by which human bodies become transformed into commercial products, I think that the records should be open to the public.

Radical transparency ushers in a different host of problems and might even decrease the overall supply of bodies. In the United Kingdom, for example, a new initiative to open the records of egg donors has practically extinguished the supply of donor eggs for couples who are unable to conceive on their own. Now British women travel to Spain and Cyprus to buy eggs.

However, the transparency ethos destroys the opportunities for brokers who will stop at nothing to acquire human bodies. No one could be killed or kidnapped for his or her kidneys if the person who bought it was able to track down the original family to send a thank-you note. No children would be kidnapped from their parents if all adoptions were open. And no blood sellers would be locked in rooms for years at a time to create an infinitesimal increase in the local blood supply.

It's time to stop ignoring red markets and start taking responsibility for them.

Superintendent Mishra (*right*) and Scott Carney (*left*) one year after Emily's death. Mishra has since been promoted and drives with an escort of two jeeps packed with machine-gun-toting foot soldiers.

CHAPTER ONE
BODY ALCHEMY

FOR A BRIEF moment Emily* is weightless, suspended between the point where the upward momentum from her limbs is about to give way to gravity. Here, at the apogee of her ascent, the physics have sealed her fate—but her body is still hers. In a moment the impact will set off a chain of events wherein Emily the person ceases to exist and the fate of her physical self will rest on others' shoulders. For now though, at the crux between going up and coming down, she is immutable. Perhaps even beautiful. As she falls the wind brushing back her hair starts to gain force.

She hits the concrete, sending echoes across the monastery's courtyard, but the handful of students who are still awake at three in the morning don't react. Earlier that night Emily was sitting

---

* Here, and in many other parts of this book, I have changed names, either at the request of my sources or to protect people from reprisals.

with them. She hadn't said much, and she wandered away without fanfare. No one connected Emily's absence to the crash in the courtyard. In India such rackets are ordinary. They didn't investigate, so her body lies still and silent in the damp blue moonlight. The students consider themselves fortunate to meditate in the spot where the Buddha attained enlightenment in India almost three thousand years ago. The city is named Bodh Gaya in his honor; the name literally translates to "where the Buddha went." For the last ten days they have been starved of speech and sitting in silent meditation in front of a golden Buddha statue. Strict prohibitions against talking have made them restless. Finally allowed use of their tongues again, they have stayed up late chattering like children on their last day of summer camp.

For an hour I sleep soundly just ten feet away from her body, covered by a white mosquito net and dreaming peacefully about returning home to my wife. Then someone jostles my shoulder and I open my eyes to the bearded face of one of my students, a New Yorker. He's panicking. "Emily's on the ground, and she's not breathing." Acting on instinct alone, I bolt upright and pull on a pair of blue jeans and a faded shirt and race out to the courtyard.

Stephanie, the other director in the program, is rolling the body over onto an orange camping pad. Emily's right eye is dark and bruised and her hair is matted with blood. Too shocked to even acknowledge my presence, Stephanie is blindly focused on trying to bring Emily back to life. She does chest compressions through Emily's red linen shirt. The contents of a medical supply bag are exploded on the dew-soaked grass with syringes and bandages strewn pell-mell. Stephanie's lips turn up into a grimace when she sees faint traces of blood well up in Emily's mouth with each press on her sternum. There is no pulse.

By now everyone in the monastery is on their feet and crowding the scene. A woman with long brown hair and an Austrian accent faints when she sees the blood. I dial the numbers for the program's founders in the United States on my cell phone to deliver the news.

After I hang up I take notes and plan phone calls to her family, while three students help load Emily into a rusted ambulance that the monastery keeps to deliver medical services to villagers in the countryside. Tonight it ferries her body across parched farmland and a bustling military cantonment in the direction of the only hospital. Emily is declared dead on arrival at Gaya Medical College on March 12, 2006, at 4:26 A.M.

By 10:26 A.M. I've aged a year. The journal she left on the balcony outside her room is full of imagery that makes me suspect suicide. Ten days of silent meditation coupled with the ordinary culture shock from visiting a country half a world away from home had not sat well with her. But the reasons for her death don't seem to matter as much as the brute force of the tasks ahead. Her home city of New Orleans is eighty-five hundred miles away; the first legs of the journey are across the parched and barren wastelands of rural India. A train accident near the rail hub in the holy city of Varanasi the night before cut the rail lines to Gaya, and the local airport seems uninterested in facilitating an airlift for a corpse.

As a red sun peeks above the horizon, two police officers in green khaki uniforms wearing semiautomatic pistols on their hips and handlebar mustaches have already seen the corpse at the hospital and have come by with questions.

"Did she have any enemies? Anyone who was jealous?" asks Superintendent Mishra, who, more than six feet tall, cuts a striking silhouette. There are two silver stars on his epaulette. He suspects murder.

"Not that I know of," I reply, frozen by the suspicion in his voice.

"Her injuries are . . ." He pauses, uncertain of his English. "Extensive."

I show him the spot where she had fallen, and the array of medical supplies and torn bits of emergency equipment left over from our failed attempt to resuscitate her. He writes something in a notebook but doesn't pursue the questioning. Instead he asks me to come to the hospital. There is something he needs me to do.

Within minutes I'm sitting in the back of a police jeep with Mishra and three young guards, barely out of their teens, who are casually holding World War II–era submachine guns. The worn silver barrel of one of the Stens points toward my belly as we bump down the road. I worry that it could go off at any moment, but I don't say anything.

Mishra turns around in the passenger seat and smiles. He seems happy to be helping an American; it's a novelty that breaks up his ordinary police work. "How do police work in America? Is it like on TV?" he asks.

I shrug. I really don't know.

Barreling down the opposite side of the road I see another SUV. Through the dust-matted windshield I make out the silhouette of a white woman with brown hair. It's Stephanie. We make eye contact as the jeeps pass each other. She looks tired.

A few minutes later we reach the crowded and potholed streets of Gaya. Although it is one of the larger cities in the state of Bihar, development is a distant dream. Despite the central government's best efforts, feudalism is still the governing policy here. The men who control the city now are the inheritors of a system that began in the times of maharajas. Giant pigs coated in black mud wander on the street sifting through trash and grunting pedestrians out of their way. Some are standing next to a butcher's shop waiting for treats. As we zoom past, the butcher splits a skinned goat's head in two and tosses the wasted bits to the swine. One sucks up a discarded intestine like it's a string of spaghetti.

Three turns later the jeep breaches the compound of Gaya medical college and stops in front of a concrete building. Bright red block letters painted on the awning announce the word CASUALTY. In the hierarchy of Indian medical institutions this school is barely an afterthought: an aberration that only attracts the country's most mediocre talent. Though it was established during colonial times when British bureaucrats ruled the land from beneath pith helmets and sunburns, the college today bears no vestiges of the imperial architecture. Instead, the campus is sprinkled with squat concrete buildings built on depleted government budgets. While much of India has forged ahead on an information-technology rocket ride, the state of Bihar is still sitting on the grandstands by the launching pad.

I hop out and Mishra leads me into the ward. A nurse in a Florence Nightingale–white uniform and hat greets me with dull eyes that are accustomed to tragedy. Opposite her on a concrete slab Emily's corpse is cooling beneath a moth-eaten wool blanket. Sometime during the night the nurse brought in a few flimsy partitions to keep away the curious. Rick, an American who volunteers at the monastery's clinic, has been waiting with her body since dark.

Mishra pulls back the shroud that has been protecting Emily from the flies and reveals her battered body. In the hours since she hit the ground the temperature of her corpse has dropped a dozen degrees and the cooling has exaggerated her injuries. A dark smear of blood stains the skin under her eye, and a bulge at the base of her neck looks like she might have broken it in the fall. Marks on her arm that were invisible when Stephanie was performing CPR are now stark and defined like military camouflage.

Mishra asks me to tell him what I see and to catalog her possessions for the police report. The police have legal custody of her body, and he's technically responsible if anything goes missing. She's wearing a linen shirt and a long skirt that she picked up in a Delhi tourist bazaar. There's a string of wooden beads around her right wrist.

"What color?" he asks, again conscious of his English.

"The shirt is *lal,* red, skirt *neela,* blue," I say. He scratches the letters onto the pad with a ballpoint pen. The injuries match her outfit.

If he is musing on the curious combination of colors, he doesn't muse long. His thoughts are interrupted by the sounds of tires crunching on gravel, announcing a new arrival.

Outside, newsmen have pulled up in two small Maruti Omni vans. Like circus clowns they spill out into the parking lot, a jumble of bodies, sound equipment, and B-grade camcorders. The reporters' existence, like the medical college's, is a testament to marginalization. In the rest of the country, news channels compete for scoops, but here, reporting is a team sport. And for today's story they share transportation, too. Sixteen people stand awkwardly around the empty vans as two producers sort gear by matching monochromatic logos on microphones to their camera counterparts.

Mishra goes out to bar their progress—or perhaps to say hello to old friends. From where I'm standing inside the ward, I can barely make out their raised voices, but I know what is coming next. I peek through the wrought-iron gate and try to catch the exact moment when a line producer palms a yellow rupee note into Superintendent Mishra's open hand. I don't see the exchange, but I know that I only have a few seconds to get ready for an interview.

I pull the hospital blanket back over her face and walk to the front of the room. A half dozen camera flashes momentarily blind me. A video crew blasts a hot yellow light that beats down on my forehead. The reporters churn a sea of microphones in front of my face and release their first salvo of questions.

"How did she die?"

"Was she murdered?"

"Was it suicide?"

And then, almost as an afterthought, "Who are you?"

The questions are sensible. But I don't answer. For the last six hours my boss in the United States has been trying to get in touch with Emily's parents, but I still don't know if they have heard the news. There is a chance that a story could appear on an American news channel before they have been tracked down.

By now the person who Emily was has been replaced by the problem that her body represents. The urgency that was present when we were trying to save her life is over, and now all there is are the inevitabilities of death. What's left of her is vulnerable. Perishable. And somehow a lot of people have a stake in her remains.

"No comment," I say, squinting my eyes against the relentless glare of the camera lights. The questions keep coming, but the urgency in the reporters' voices is fading. A gleam in one cameraman's eye tells me that they are angling for a shot of her corpse. I raise my arm in front of his lens, but a man in a red polo shirt grabs my arm and tries to push me away. I pull against him, but it's a lost cause. He lets go and I spin wide. Within a second they are past me and pulling back the shroud that had been covering her face.

Under the light's harsh glare, the blood under her eye stands out dark and purple. The wound traces its way through a crack in her skull and back to her brain. On Indian television death has a starring role right next to diamond-dripping Bollywood celebrities. Tasteful shots of covered bodies and toe tags are for American newspapers. Instead, on the Indian news the faces of the dead loll obscenely, shot after grotesque shot, in unending montages of personal tragedy. India's dead aren't camera shy. If it is my duty to protect Emily, I have failed.

This evening, news-flash updates across the country will read:

American student dies at Bodh Gaya meditation center.
Police suspect murder or suicide.

American's don't die in India every day. Today she will be more famous for being a dead body than for the person she was alive. For the time that it takes for one news item to transmute into another, the national attention will be on this spot. A billion people will have a chance to see her lifeless face.

I push my way back in front of the cameras but the reporters already have begun to wrap up. They have what they need.

Officer Mishra is balancing a hefty cane in his left hand. His face is a kaleidoscope of looks that say simultaneously, "Your five hundred rupees are up" and "I don't know how these guys got past me." Not that it matters to the reporters who have already begun to file out and get into the waiting vans. The drivers gun the engines and they race off to the meditation center to get a peek at the crime scene.

The room, a circus a minute ago, is now as silent as a tomb. I have nothing to do but resume my vigil. Mishra offers me a smile and a shrug and goes back to his post outside. Alone again with Emily's corpse, a new reality begins to settle in. Not only has a student of mine died tragically in one of the remotest areas of India, but now I need to get her body back home. Six hours after her death, very little separates the empty husk she left behind from a poorly packaged slab of meat. And with the temperature threatening to reach 100 degrees by noon, there isn't much time to halt the process of decay.

At the front desk of the hospital the nurse in the Florence Nightingale uniform tells me that the hospital doesn't have an ice machine. What's more, I can't even take possession of her body until after a government-mandated autopsy. She suggests that I sit with the body until the doctors arrive.

I wait.

Eventually a small ambulance that is the same make and model of the van that the journalists used pulls up outside the ward. The only difference between the vehicles is that the rear seats of this one have been removed in favor of a rack for a gurney. Two men wearing rumpled button-down business shirts and threadbare slacks say that they have come to take the body for an autopsy.

They drop her into the back of the van with a dull thump and drive half a mile down the dirt road. I sit with the body in the back as they forge their way across campus and finally pull up outside a small, dilapidated, government building with gaping holes in its aluminum roof. A sign on its door in Hindi reads POSTMORTEM CLASSROOM. The room looks like it hasn't been used in a decade. There are several rows of seats on elevated platforms, presumably so students can get a better view of the dissection. Some of the chairs in the middle rows have been upended, and the space is covered in dust and pigeon droppings. At the front of the class are a slate chalkboard and a massive obsidian table that is cool to the touch. They drop Emily's corpse on the table and padlock the door.

"The doctors will be here soon," they say before retreating behind a corner to smoke small hand-rolled cigarettes. I notice discarded clothing and several large clumps of hair outside the building—apparently scraps left over from previous autopsies.

When they're done with their *beedies,* one of them brings me to a nearby building, this one much larger than the postmortem classroom. Here, they say, the superintendent of the medical college will be waiting to meet me. When I arrive Dr. Das is wringing his hands over an impressive amount of paperwork and his jet-black toupee is slightly off-kilter.

The doctor works double duty running the daily affairs of the college and conducting autopsies for the police. When classes are in session he teaches incoming medical students the ins and outs of forensic analysis. That sometimes means reenacting wounds on the unclaimed corpses that come through his morgue. It's a popular course. And it explains why there are four cabinets full of deadly poisons as well as potential murder weapons, running the gamut from swords, daggers, and machetes to screwdrivers and cricket bats with nails driven through them. Resting on the bottom shelf of the cabinet is a sheaf of crime-scene photos with dead bodies in different stages of decay. As we speak he occasionally gazes at a medical skeleton hanging in the window.

"This is a very special case," he begins. "Not many foreigners die in this city, so we have to be very careful with how we proceed. Many people are watching."

As a student, Emily was just one of a handful of young American women in Indian dress perusing holy sites on a spiritual journey. Dead, she is a burgeoning international incident echoing through police bureaucracies, embassy corridors, and insurance companies charged with doling out tens of thousands of dollars to repatriate her remains.

And everything, I learn, hinges on Dr. Das's report of her death. If he determines that the injuries on her body indicate a possible murder, bureaucratic rules dictate that Emily's body may have to remain in police custody until the investigation is complete. However, since his medical school has no facilities to preserve a body for more than a few days, keeping her here will mean that she will decompose to a point where the airlines will refuse to airlift her body out of the country.

On the other hand, if he reports that her death is a suicide, the police case can close quickly. But her family, he explains, which by now must know about her death, is Catholic and will not accept that she took her own life only to burn in hell for all of eternity. In fact, they may demand an extra investigation to prove some other cause of death. He's shaking his head slowly.

"You see, it is a dilemma," he says, concerned. "It would have been easier had she not died at all."

There is an imperceptibly thin line that separates live flesh from dead. And the problem with dying is that once that line has been crossed all the rules around how we deal with a person's physical presence change. Dr. Das sighs and looks across the room to an attendant holding two empty mason jars.

"Perhaps it is time that we begin." He pushes his palms against his desk and lifts himself heavily. Grabbing a black medical bag, he goes into the hallway, leaving me alone with the cabinets full of medical curiosities.

I don't follow him. Instead I look at the cricket bat with a rusty nail hammered through the end hanging inside one of his gruesome bookcases. The nail's tip is bent and a ring of crusted blood sticks lightly to the wood. I shudder to think about the wound that Dr. Das inflicted on an unclaimed corpse. Then, as if I had forgotten it was there at all, my phone begins to vibrate in my pocket.

At the other end of the line, half a world away through a sea of buzzes and crackles, comes the voice of the program's director in New York. "Scott? I have a favor to ask."

TWO DAYS LATER, A low orange sun surfaces lazily above the Gangetic Plain and begins its slow ascent across the sky. It's early, but I didn't sleep. My eyes are rimmed red with exhaustion. I spent two days searching the city for a reliable source of ice to keep Emily's body cool. With the help of the monastery, I dropped hundreds of pounds of ice into her coffin, which we had made at a wood-shop. I made every effort to avoid seeing her body when I did so. Together we have moved the body two more times: from the postmortem chamber back to the monastery, and finally to a small morgue that hospital administrators had neglected to mention existed when this all began.

Forensic experts in the United States don't trust their Indian counterparts, so my boss in New York asked me to take pictures of Emily's corpse to send back for independent analysis. I'm holding a digital camera that I borrowed from a student. Though she has already had an autopsy here, results are never certain. Without taking pictures I've been told that the family may raise an objection, and the body might never leave India.

A police jeep picks me up at my hotel and I drive to the medical college. I'm sitting next to a police officer armed with a submachine gun. His head tilts backward and his eyes flutter between sleep and wakefulness. He doesn't seem to notice that the barrel is pointed right at my abdomen again. I've been here before, I think to myself. A half hour later the cop is still sleeping when we arrive at the postmortem classroom. It's padlocked shut, and a grizzled attendant wrestles with the keys; his fingers seem to shake uncontrollably. He suggests that a hundred rupees would steady his hand.

I try to brace myself. I expect to be repulsed. The prospect of seeing her postautopsied corpse scares me. A dead body is one thing, but looking at someone after they have been processed by surgeons makes me wonder if they have taken out more than just her organs—whether something more vital might be missing. Bile churns in my stomach.

A minute later, I'm inside and staring at her laid out on a metal gurney.

The doctors have split her down the middle with crude tools—opening her wide from the base of her neck to her pelvis. They broke her ribs to see her heart. To access her brain the doctors sawed a lateral gash through her forehead and skull. They peeled the skin of her face back onto itself. Her forehead was folded over her eyes and the scalp pulled backward. As expected, they saw blood pooled inside her skull. The pressure of that blood against her brain was enough to kill her.

But the surgeons didn't stop there. They cut out pieces of her liver, brain, heart, and kidney to rule out poisoning. To determine if she had been raped, they removed portions of her vagina, cervix, and fallopian tubes. They gathered all the organs together into three large mason jars and marked them "viscera." A courier then took the jars to a laboratory three hundred kilometers away. They stitched her up with broad, inelegant sutures.

The findings were as brutal as the procedure. The official cause of death listed in the autopsy report read: "Shock and hemorrhage due to head injury. The injuries simulate a fall from height."

I don't feel the way I had anticipated. A different, and perhaps more disturbing, emotion creeps up my stomach and flushes my cheeks.

I'm embarrassed.

Her injuries don't disturb me. I'm more prepared for those than I had thought. It's her nakedness that fills me with regret.

Alive, Emily was a beautiful twenty-one-year-old woman in the prime of her life. She could make other girls jealous with her grace, athletic frame, and poise without even knowing it. Having studied yoga for years, her body was at the peak of physical health, with toned muscles and flawless skin. The Emily I knew was strong and in control of her own surroundings.

But here, naked and dead, I know more about Emily than I ever wanted to. When she slides out of the machine, both the attendant and I share an intimate view that would only have been the domain of her lovers. The smell of her viscera, mixed with some preserving agent, is almost palpable in the air; the transgression of her legs, hips, breasts, and stomach seems like it should be forbidden. But the dead don't have secrets. Emily's privacy evaporated the moment she stopped breathing. She crossed over to another world where the laws and customs that govern her are different from what they were a week ago. In this world, her parents need photos of their naked daughter. Here she doesn't flinch when men study, identify, and puzzle over her insides. Whether we acknowledge it or not, our most intimate relationship in life is the one we have with our own bodies. The final indignity of death is losing that control.

The shell of her body is less than the body she was born and grew up with. The injuries damaged her frame, but the far more aggressive harvesting by the college's pathologists has carved her to pieces and then sent those pieces across the state. This is the body that we will tell stories about and that her parents will weep over. But to call what is left of her "Emily," or even "Emily's body," is a lie. Whatever this is, it is incomplete and will never be whole again.

There is a strange transmutation that we play on the dead. Here on this table, her skin is a bag, the valuable bits already removed, the brisk sutures zipping up her empty cavity. In death she is an object to be parceled and given out to any stakeholder who lays a claim, from the reporters who sold her image to the networks, to the doctors who cut her, to the parents who want to claim her whole. Now I am part of that chain, too: a collector and storyteller for (of?) the dead. Emily, whoever she was, is lost; these are just her parts. It is the same story for everybody. Every body.

I check the light meter and set the camera to harvest. The shutter slams against the frame as I snap pictures in rapid succession: starting at her toes I cover every inch of her until I reach the gash on her forehead. In a little under an hour she will be on a plane to Delhi. From there her body will travel to Louisiana, where she will be buried wearing a light-blue sari that her parents will buy specially for her interment. An attendant comes in to pick up her corpse and load it into a waiting van. I know that part of me will never leave this room.

The only way to preserve Emily's body after she died in Bodh Gaya in March 2006 was to pack her coffin in ice and then fly the corpse to Delhi. This photo was taken upon the flight's arrival in Delhi.

This cache of bones was confiscated from the banks of a river and now sits in a dilapidated evidence locker in Purbasthali, West Bengal, India. The bones had been stolen from grave sites by a group of skeleton traders who sell the remains to American anatomical supply companies. The Indian parliament criminalized the trade in human bones in 1985, but people still make money on human remains. The more than one hundred skulls in this seizure would be worth more than $70,000 on the American market.

CHAPTER TWO
THE BONE FACTORY

A CONSTABLE IN a sweat-stained undershirt and checkered blue sarong jerks open the back door of a decrepit Indian-made Tata Sumo SUV—what passes for an evidence locker at this rustic police outpost in the Indian state of West Bengal. A hundred human skulls tumble out onto a ragged cloth covering a patch of mud, making a hollow clatter as they fall to the ground. They've lost most of their teeth bouncing around in the back of the truck. Bits of bone and enamel scatter like snowflakes around the growing pile.

Standing next to the truck, the ranking officer smiles, clasps his hands over his bulging belly, and lets out a satisfied grunt. "Now you can see how big the bone business is here," he says. I crouch down and pick up a skull. It's lighter than I expected. I hold it up to my nose. It smells like fried chicken.

Before the authorities intercepted it, this cache was moving along a well-established pipeline for human skeletal remains. For

150 years, India's bone trade has followed a route from remote Indian villages to the world's most distinguished medical schools. The tentacles of the network stretch across the state and into neighboring countries. I'd seen similar caches on the border of Bhutan that were destined for a different market, but these are the real thing: meticulously prepared medical specimens.

Skeletons aren't easy to get. In the United States, for instance, most corpses receive a prompt burial or cremation. Bodies donated to science usually end up on the dissection table or their bones sawed to pieces. Sometimes they're sucked into the more profitable industry of medical grafts. So most complete skeletons used for medical study come from overseas. Often they arrive without the informed consent of their former owners and in violation of the laws of their country of origin.

For almost two hundred years India has been the world's primary source of bones used in medical study, renowned for producing specimens scrubbed to a pristine white patina and fitted with high-quality connecting hardware. In 1985, however, the Indian government outlawed the export of human remains, and the global supply of skeletons collapsed. Western countries turned to China and Eastern Europe, but those regions export relatively few skeletons. They have little experience producing display-quality specimens, and their products are regarded as inferior.

Now, more than two decades after India's export ban, there are open signs that the trade never ended. Red-market vendors in West Bengal continue to supply human skeletons and skulls using the time-honored method: rob graves, separate soft flesh from unyielding calcium, and deliver the bones to distributors—who assemble them and ship them to dealers around the globe.

Exports to North America are small compared with pre-ban levels, but that just means that it costs more for skeletons—not that they are impossible to come by. Suppliers have ample incentive—it's a lucrative business. The skulls on the ground before me, for instance, would fetch an estimated $70,000 overseas.

The constable grabs the cloth by its corners and gathers the evidence into a bundle. "You know, I've never seen anything like this," he says. "I hope I don't again."

A DAY LATER, A massive low-pressure system over the Bay of Bengal is threatening to flood the eastern armpit of India, the state of West Bengal. Newspapers have already dubbed the storm a "watery apocalypse" after eight people drowned in floods before it even touched land. I'm driving to the tiny village of Purbasthali—about eighty miles outside of Kolkata, the state capital, which was renamed from Calcutta in 2001. The village is the site of the processing plant where the police discovered their load of skulls. My rented Toyota Qualis gets stuck in the mud half a mile from the facility, so I jump out to make my way on foot. The sky is pitch-black, the rain suffocating. Toads the size of boxing gloves hop across the muddy track.

When police arrived to investigate in early 2007, they could smell the stench of rotting flesh from nearly a mile away. Sections of spine strung together with twine dangled from the rafters, an officer told me. Hundreds of bones were scattered on the floor in some sort of ordering system.

This bone factory had been operating for more than one hundred years when two of its workers, drinking at a bar, bragged that they were hired to dig bodies out of graves. Shocked villagers dragged them to a police station, where they confessed. The workers said a man named Mukti Biswas ran the factory. The authorities knew him well. In 2006 police had arrested Biswas as the kingpin of a grave-robbing ring; he was released a day later, news reports said, "because of his political links." The police took him into custody once again, but, in accordance with precedent, he was let out on bail and has since taken flight.

AFTER TEN MINUTES OF slogging through the mud, I make out the flicker of a gas lamp. I peek into the doorway of a wood-framed house. A family of four sitting on the dirt floor stares back at me.

"Do you know Mukti Biswas?" I ask.

"The bastard still owes me money," replies Manoj Pal, a twenty-something man with a thin mustache. His family has been working at the bone factory for generations—just as long as Biswas has owned it—he says. He offers to show me around, and we head out along the bank of the Bhagirathi River.

The processing plant is little more than a bamboo hut with a tarpaulin roof—one of more than a dozen bone factories Pal says he knows about. In April the authorities confiscated piles of bones, buckets of hydrochloric acid, and two barrels full of a caustic chemical they have yet to identify. All that's left is a dirt floor with a large concrete vat sunk into the ground.

A third-generation bone trader, Biswas had no problem finding dead bodies. As caretaker of the village's cremation ground, he claimed to have a license to dispose of the dead. But police told reporters that he was robbing graves instead. Biswas pilfered corpses from cemeteries, morgues, and funeral pyres; he would drag the deceased from the flames as soon as the families left. He employed almost a dozen people to shepherd the bones through the various stages of defleshing and curing. For this work, Pal says he earned $1.25 a day. He also received a bonus for keeping the bones from a given body together so they represented a biological individual rather than a mishmash of parts—a feature prized by doctors.

Pal explains the factory's production process. First the corpses are wrapped in netting and anchored in the river, where bacteria and fish reduce them to loose piles of bones and mush in a week or so. The crew then scrubs the bones and boils them in a cauldron of water and caustic soda to dissolve any remaining flesh. That leaves the calcium surfaces with a yellow tint. To bring them up to medical white, bones are then left in sunlight for a week before being soaked in hydrochloric acid.

Biswas had customers across Kolkata. Many skeletons made their way to the grisly wards of the anatomy department at Calcutta Medical College, where local Doms, a traditional grave-tending caste, would pay him in cash. The skeletons are required materials for the hundreds of local medical students who graduate every year. But he also sold complete skeletons wholesale for $45 to a medical supply company called Young Brothers, which wired the pieces together, painted on medical diagrams, and sawed away sections of the skulls to reveal their internal structures. Then Young Brothers sold the bones to dealers around the world.*

Shining my flashlight on the floor, I pick up a wet rag. The translator lets out a low hiss. "I hope you know that's a death shroud," he says. I drop the cloth and wipe my hand on my shirt.

I'd been pursuing Mukti Biswas through a cell phone number I took from a local reporter for a week and a half before I actually made contact. Over the crackling connection he says that the police have chosen to banish him rather than prosecute his case. The only way he will meet me is with their permission and, preferably, with the local superintendent in the room. To do otherwise could make the cops reconsider their leniency.

I wait for him as rain pounds on the clay roof tiles of the Purbasthali police outpost while the cop in charge offers me endless cups of tea. Out the window I can see the chemicals that the bone factory used to process skeletons sitting in a couple of metal drums. Eventually the round beams of a British-era ambassador car slice through the darkness, and a chubby young man in his twenties opens the door and dashes for the station's entrance. It isn't him. Mukti has decided to stay in hiding. He has sent his son instead.

"This was no secret. It's been a family business for as long as I can remember," he says in his father's defense. He explains that someone has to run the burning ghats or there will be no way to dispose of the dead.

---

* There is a double standard in Indian law that allows local medical students to study bones that were robbed from graves; however, it is illegal to sell those same bones to foreigners. This is because the law that legislated away the bone business was essentially a trade law, not a criminal one. It would make more sense to ban the practice altogether.

What about robbing graves? "I don't know anything about that," he replies.

VICTIMS, HOWEVER, ARE NOT hard to find.

Mohammed Mullah Box, a gaunt man in his seventies, is the caretaker of a small burial ground in the village of Harbati. When the dead go missing, he's the first person that grieving relatives come to for answers. Today he doesn't have any answers or bodies. As he sits on the edge of an empty grave, a tear rolls down from one of his wrinkled eyes and spills onto his cheek.

A few weeks ago, robbers sneaked into the graveyard and exhumed the remains of one of his neighbors shortly after the body had been buried. By now, the skeleton is probably hanging in a Kolkata warehouse, ready to be shipped out to a dealer in the Western world.

I ask Box whether he fears what might happen to his own body when he dies.

"Of course," he says.

THE EMPIRICAL STUDY OF human anatomy took off with Leonardo da Vinci's sketches in the fifteenth century; the earliest known articulated skeleton dates from 1543. As medicine advanced, physicians were expected to have a systematic understanding of the human body's inner workings. By the beginning of the nineteenth century, Europe's demand for human remains far outstripped the supply.

In England, home of many of the world's preeminent medical institutions, grave robbing became so commonplace that cer-

tain cemeteries were famous for battles between grieving families
and marauding medical students. But the situation was perhaps
even direr in the United States, where the medical industry was
expanding at a faster rate than the population. In 1760 there
were five medical schools in all of America. Just one hundred
years later the total boomed to sixty-five. Early Americans suf-
fered from a broad range of diseases that gave medical institutions brisk business. The moneymaking opportunities meant
that becoming a doctor could be a test case for the American
dream. There was no class bar to opening a medical practice; all
that was necessary to become a doctor was a solid education and
determined hard work.

Throughout the 1800s, medical schools saw incoming classes
with freshmen eager to get their hands dirty. But corpses—raw
materials for study—were scarce. The historian Michael Sappol
notes in *A Traffic in Dead Bodies,* his landmark tome on nineteenth-century resurrectionists, as grave robbers were known, that
anatomy rooms were sites of camaraderie where doctors forged
their identity as medical professionals. They learned and bonded
in the labs as they reduced stolen dead bodies to component pieces.
The budding doctors enjoyed lively gallows humor: numerous
reports describe doctors posing dramatically with corpses and
waving severed limbs out medical school windows at perplexed
and distraught pedestrians.

Body snatching itself was a rite of passage. In 1851 the *Boston
Medical & Surgical Journal* devoted twenty-one pages, almost its
entire issue, to the career of Dr. Charles Knowlton. In that tract
the author praised skulduggery, writing, "the risk of exhumation
is to them trifling, when compared to the advantages of a labored

investigation of the human frame by the dissection knife. Their thirst for the acquisition of knowledge is as ardent and craving as the appetite of a drunkard. It is to such spirits as these that our profession owes its elevated rank."*

Grave robbing didn't go down well with the community at large, so doctors followed basic rules to keep complaints to a minimum. Except in rare cases corpses were not typically stolen from upper-class or primarily white graveyards. Where possible, they dissected black—or in a pinch, Irish—corpses, the lowest rungs on the American social ladder. In part that was a practical response to changing American and European funerary traditions that made dying a high-security event. Body snatching was so commonplace that wealthy graveyards posted sentries, raised formidable walls, and dug deeper trenches than the graveyards of the poor. Funeral parlors sold heavy concrete monuments to placed above caskets in order to impede digging. Some funeral homes even offered anti–body snatching alarms that triggered when a robber's shovel breeched the burial vault.

Authorities, however, were willing to overlook the crime of grave robbing by the medical community as a necessary evil. Doctors needed dead bodies if they wanted to make living ones healthy. Arrests were rare and only targeted the lowly grave robbers who did it for profit—not the medical schools who hired them or the medical student who dug up bodies for free.

With authorities unwilling to intervene on the plundering

---

* Michael Sappol, "The Odd Case of Charles Knowlton: Anatomical Performance, Medical Narrative, and Identity in Antebellum America," *Bulletin of the History of Medicine* 83, no. 3 (2009): 467.

doctors, the public's outrage turned to vigilante justice. Between 1765 and 1884 there were twenty anatomy riots across America. While each riot had slightly different roots, they were generally spontaneous public outcries prompted when body snatchers were caught in the act, or by chance when a visitor saw someone he knew on the dissection table.

Riots of the era seemed to have inspired the climactic scene in *Frankenstein*. Crowds often formed in graveyards where they could see the empty graves for themselves and then proceeded to medical schools, where they threw rocks and brandished torches. Their goal was to destroy the offending anatomy labs. But they weren't effective in quelling the practice. In several cases the only way to subdue the riots was to call in the state militia and fire into the mob, inevitably leaving several more fresh bodies in the graveyards. In a way, the riots were just another cost of doing business.

Outrage over body snatching was generally short-lived and burned out with the destruction of property. It would take more than mobs of angry citizens to spark real government reform. That had to wait until two Irish immigrants in Scotland hatched a plan to supply an unlimited number of bodies to the University of Edinburgh.

William Hare owned a run-down boardinghouse in the town of West Port. Occasionally a tenant would die without paying rent and he would be left with cleaning up the mess. While he was carting the body of one of his broke and recently deceased tenants to the graveyard, a doctor intercepted him and offered £10 for it. He also said he would offer a similar fee for any other body that Hare could turn up. Hare quickly enrolled the services of another tenant,

William Burke, and the two embarked on a killing spree that lasted a year and claimed the lives of seventeen victims. The crimes were so gruesome and so captivated the public imagination that the story was retold in countless newspaper and penny magazine articles of the time. The tale continues to inspire films in this century.

Mostly in response to the Burke and Hare murders, England passed the Anatomy Act of 1832. The act severely limited body snatching in England by allowing doctors to claim any unclaimed corpse left in a city morgue or hospital. Similar measures were adopted in America.

The act came just in the nick of time. Besides being study aids, by the turn of the century, anatomical skeletons were becoming popular decorations and status symbols for American and European doctors. They were presented as a sign of medical competence in the same ways that stethoscopes and medical school diplomas are today.

According to Sappol, the skeletons either purposely lacked information about their provenance, or clearly indicated that hanging skeletons came from "executed negros," to reassure patrons that the "funerary honor of members of the white community had not been violated."*

The only problem was that black executed prisoners were in short supply. So British doctors looked to their colonies. In India members of the Dom caste, who traditionally performed cremations, were pressed into processing bones. By the 1850s, Calcutta

---

* Michael Sappol, *A Traffic in Dead Bodies* (Princeton: Princeton University Press. 2002), 94.

Medical College was churning out nine hundred skeletons a year, mostly for shipment abroad. A century later, a newly independent India dominated the market in human bones.

In 1985 the *Chicago Tribune* reported that India had exported sixty thousand skulls and skeletons the year before. The supply was sufficient for every medical student in the developed world to buy a bone box along with their textbooks for just $300.[*]

If most of the merchandise was stolen, at least exporting it was legal. "For years, we ran everything aboveboard," Bimalendu Bhattacharjee, a former president of the Indian Association of Exporters of Anatomical Specimens, told the *Los Angeles Times* in 1991. "No one advertised, but everyone knew it was going on." At their height, Kolkata's bone factories took in an estimated $1 million a year.[†]

Another major supplier, the Reknas Company, sold thousands of skeletons to Kilgore International in Minnesota. The current owner, Craig Kilgore, remembers that at the time there was never any talk about grave robbing. "We were told that overpopulation was such a big problem that people would just die where they slept and carts would pick up the dead bodies off the street," he says.

Pictures of the (now-defunct) Reknas factory floor show a full-blown operation of lab-coat-wearing professionals assembling entire skeleton families. In the golden era of the skeleton trade,

---

[*] Mark Fineman, "A Serene, Spiritual Mecca Has Become a Nation of Assassins," *Chicago Tribune,* September 27, 1985.

[†] Mark Fineman, "Living Off the Dead Is a Dying Trade in Calcutta," *Los Angeles Times,* February 19, 1991.

the export houses were among the most prestigious employment options in the city. Like doctors in colonial America, the skeleton industry was a path to success with a low bar of entry. The industry was also supported by the city, which issued licenses to skeleton dealers. Not only were they taking care of the unclaimed dead, they were providing a valuable revenue stream for a city that the rest of India thought was past its heyday.

But the profits couldn't last without covering up a dirty secret. Simply collecting the corpses of destitute people and from the local morgues wasn't enough. Some companies tried to increase the supply by buying bodies before death, offering a small purse of cash to people who promised to donate their corpses when they had passed on. But attempts for a willed donation program were too slow and unreliable. A company that worked like that could take years to get a particular skeleton, while fresh bodies were being set into soil and were ripe for the taking. Just like colonial America and the United Kingdom, skeleton supply companies saw grave robbing as the only solution. History was about to repeat itself.

The West's unquenchable appetite for skeletons meant that West Bengal's graveyards were being picked clean, and the lure of ready money soon attracted criminal elements. In an event that mirrored the murders by Burke and Hare, the industry shuddered to a halt in March 1985, when a bone trader was arrested after exporting fifteen hundred children's skeletons. Because they're relatively rare and illustrate transitional stages in osteological development, children's skeletons command higher prices than adult ones. Indian newspapers claimed that children were being kidnapped and killed for their bones.

Panic spread with news of the arrest. In the months after the indictment, vigilantes combed the cities searching for members of the alleged kidnappers' network. In September of that year, an Australian tourist was killed and a Japanese tourist beaten by a mob after rumors spread that they were involved in the conspiracy. The attacks themselves might have been enough to stall India's bone industry, but the government had already taken action: A few weeks earlier, India's Supreme Court interpreted the national Import/Export Control Act to prohibit the export of human tissue.

In the absence of competing suppliers in other countries, the court's decision effectively shut down international trade in human skeletons. Medical schools in the United States and Europe begged the Indian government to reverse the export ban to no avail.

Since then, natural human bone has been difficult to come by. The voracious demand for fresh cadavers in medical education consumes nearly all donated corpses in the United States, and in any case, processing skeletons is a slow, messy business that few people care to take on. When high-quality specimens do become available, they tend to be costly. A complete skeleton in good condition now retails for several thousand dollars, and orders can take months, even years, to fulfill. Students no longer buy their own bone boxes; instead, schools usually keep an inventory that's replaced only when specimens are damaged or stolen. Stanford Medical School allocates half a skeleton, cleaved down the middle, for every two students. Such policies mean that many established institutions already have all the bones they need. The biggest buyers of skeletons are new and growing schools throughout the world that need to outfit their labs. Many medical schools around the developing world, most notably Pakistan and China, still source their bones from local grave-yards—occasionally risking public ire. But large-scale exports have dwindled.

In the United States some institutions have turned to plastic replicas. But artificial substitutes aren't ideal. "Plastic models are reproductions of a single specimen and don't include the range of variations found in real osteology," says Samuel Kennedy, who stocks the anatomy program at Harvard Medical School. Students trained on facsimiles never see these differences. Moreover, the models aren't entirely accurate. "The molding process doesn't cap-ture the detail of a real specimen," Kennedy adds. "This is espe-cially critical in the skull."

In the United States, major dealers like Kilgore International who made a fortune when importing skeletons was legal are now making do selling replicas. "My father would have done almost anything to get back into the bone business," says Craig Kilgore, who runs the company his father founded. "He was legally blind but would still come to the office and write letters to anyone, any-where in the world, that he felt could be of help to reopen the supply."

Some of those letters found unlikely homes. Shortly after the ban, while investigating potential new sources of bones in famine-plagued regions of Africa, a bone dealer in Nigeria told him about warehouses full of bones that were ready for export. For $50,000 he would have a near-unlimited source of human materials. The only problem was that the money would have to be delivered in cash. In Lagos.

Too old to go on his own, Charles Kilgore recruited his son, Craig, to get on a plane and meet the dealers at the Hilton Hotel.

His contact convinced him to get in a car with him and drive to the outskirts of the city to an abandoned warehouse district that bordered the jungle. "A person could go into that jungle and probably never come out," he recalled.

Worried that it was a setup, he started using the names of bones that he was interested in by the wrong terms; the distributors he was with didn't bother to correct him. Sensing danger, Kilgore convinced the purported dealers that the money was in another location and that they would have to drop him off so that he could retrieve it. When his associates were out of sight, he took a cab to the airport and caught the next plane out of town. Even though Kilgore and several other domestic skeleton importers scoured the world for new sources of bones, they were never able to find any, and the industry fell into a steep decline.

Craig's father, who died in 1995, didn't live to see the reemergence of the trade.

TUCKED AWAY ON A side street between one of Kolkata's largest graveyards and one of its busiest hospitals, Young Brothers' headquarters looks more like an abandoned warehouse than a leading distributor of human skeletons. The rusted front gate appears to have been padlocked and forgotten a decade ago. Above the entrance, the company sign is a tableau of peeling paint.

It wasn't always this way. The building was bustling with activity in 2001, according to former Kolkata Health Department chief and head of West Bengal's opposition party Javed Ahmed Khan. At the time, neighbors complained that the Young Brothers offices stank of death. Huge piles of bones lay drying on the roof. Part Eliot Ness and part Ralph Nader, Khan is the sort of politician who has no patience for police inaction and is happy to take the law into his own hands. His tactics can be brutal and have landed him in jail on several occasions—like the time in 2007 when he assaulted a doctor in a medical school who was accused of raping one of his constituents.

In 2001, when the police refused to file a case against Young Brothers, Khan raided the building with a posse of bamboo-wielding heavies. It was a version of vigilante justice that would have been familiar in nineteenth-century England and America.

"There were two rooms full of human skeletons," Khan told me. It took five trucks to haul them away. He also seized thousands of documents, including invoices to companies all around the world. "They were sending shipments to Thailand, Brazil, Europe, and the United States," he says.

Sixteen years after the export ban, it was as if the law had never taken effect. I meet Khan in the back room of a deserted boathouse. He introduces me to a young woman wearing a colorful headscarf who was employed as a clerk for Young Brothers between 1999 and 2001. "We used to fill orders all over the world. We used to buy bones from Mukti Biswas. I saw more than five thousand dead bodies," she says. She requests anonymity in case of reprisal. The company took in roughly $15,000 a month from abroad, and she tells me that Biswas's operation was just one of many. There were other suppliers and factories up and down the length of West Bengal.

Khan's raid prompted the police to arrest Young Brothers' owner, Vinesh Aron. He spent two nights in jail, but just like Mukti, he was released without charges.

. . . .

TODAY, THERE ARE NO bones on the roof. I've been poking around the area for an hour or so, interviewing neighbors, when a white van pulls up to the building. A man dressed in a pink-checkered shirt steps out. He walks briskly to a side door and knocks: Vinesh Aron.

Aron sees me snapping photos and knocks more forcefully, but his assistant inside is having trouble with the lock. As I try to quickly formulate a question, my translator shoves a microphone in his face and asks whether he's still shipping skeletons to the West. Looking flustered, Aron blurts out, "We won that case!" The entrance cracks open and he slips in before the door slams in my face.

In a subsequent phone conversation, Aron says he now sells medical models and charts, but no bones. However, a month later I meet a vendor of surgical instrument supplies who claims to be Aron's brother-in-law; he says Young Brothers is the only bone distributor in the country. Behind the counter of his small shop in Chennai are several cardboard boxes full of rare bones. He pulls a fist-sized skull of a fetus out of one box and smiles like he is holding a rare gem. "My brother-in-law is the only man who still does this in India. He is the only one with guts," he says. Then he offers to dig up a skeleton for me for ₹1,000 ($25).

The 2006–2007 Young Brothers catalog takes care to inform customers that it abides by the law. It lists a wide assortment of bones at wholesale prices, noting that they're "for sale in India only." Yet Indian skeletons are somehow making it out of the country anyway.

In Canada, Osta International sells human bones throughout the United States and Europe. The forty-year-old company offers to fill orders immediately. "About half of our business is in the States," says Christian Ruediger, who runs the business with his father, Hans.

Ruediger admits that Osta stocks bones from India, presumably smuggled out of the country in violation of the export law. Until a few years ago, he got them from a distributor in Paris, but that source dried up in 2001—around the time Javed Khan raided Young Brothers. Since then, he has bought his stock from a middleman in Singapore. He declines to provide the name. "We want to keep a low profile," he says.

Of some thirty institutions I contacted in the course of research, the handful that admitted to buying bones in the past few years declined to reveal their sources or speak on record—though Osta's name did come up twice. "I bought a complete skeleton and a dissected human demonstration skull from Osta," a professor at a prestigious Virginia college says. "Both were excellent."

Another Osta customer is a firm called Dentsply Rinn, which offers a plastic model head containing a real skull, used for training dentists. "It's very difficult to procure human bones," marketing manager Kimberly Brown says. "Our requirements stipulate that the skulls must be of a certain size and grade and without certain anatomical defects. But we have no requirement for their origin." The skull is a bestseller in both the United States and the United Kingdom.

Indian authorities express a similar lack of concern. Although the international bone trade violates the national export law and local statutes against grave desecration, officials look the other way. "This is not a new thing," says Rajeev Kumar, West Bengal's deputy inspector general of police. "There's no evidence that they were killing people." The police took an interest in Biswas only because the bodies of a few important people went missing. "We are trying to implement the law based on the stress society places on it," he adds. "Society does not see this as a very serious thing."

The need to study human bones in medicine is well established. The need to obtain the informed consent of people whose bones are studied is not. The reemergence of India's bone trade reflects the tension between these requirements. While the supply of human skeletons targets the recently dead, the even more dangerous practice of collecting living kidneys from slum dwellers is merely a modern incarnation of an ancient Indian practice.

Meanwhile, the bone factories of Kolkata are back in business.

The outside of Young Brothers, an anatomical supply company in Kolkata, India. Witnesses said that this run-down office building was a center of the Indian red market in human bones after the 1985 ban. The workers here used to dry human bones on the roof and clean the corpses of their flesh inside. The office is still active, but it is difficult to know what happens behind its closed doors.

Kala Arumugam shows a long scar along her abdomen where surgeons extracted her kidney. Although the surgery took place several months before this photo was taken, she still has trouble working. She earned $1,000 for selling her organ.

CHAPTER THREE
KIDNEY PROSPECTING

THE DAY AFTER Christmas 2004, an earthquake occurred off the coast of Banda Ache, Indonesia, sending shockwaves racing across the ocean floor and culminating in a massive burst of energy that smashed into the shores of India and Sri Lanka. The tsunami claimed more than two hundred thousand lives and left a cataclysmic wake of families torn apart and a seemingly endless stream of refugees. While NGOs and governments poured aid into the area to rebuild the lives of victims, a few entrepreneurial hospitals and organ brokers saw the tragedy as an opportunity to make a fortune peddling the kidneys of refugees.

In Tsunami Nagar, a desperately poor refugee camp for tsunami survivors in India's Tamil Nadu province, Maria Selvam is the most respected man. For two years this former fisherman has spent most of his days arguing with government bureaucrats for basic resources that had been promised to them by the international community. All he wants is for the people in the three settlements that he presides over to once again be able to make their livings from the sea. When I meet him almost two years after the tsunami, the camp is little more than a holding area with hopeless concrete rows of dismal houses. Raw sewage runs in the gutters by people's homes, and employment prospects are as scarce as the resident children's access to education.

As the village's only elected official, Selvam is the closest thing the refugees have to a celebrity. His photograph is plastered on the sides of buildings and above the wide iron gate that is the camp's official entrance. But his popularity has begun to wane. Local youths have thrown rocks through his posters and carved away the eyeballs from the images on their walls. His crime: Trying to stop the flow of organs out of Tsunami Nagar.

"It used to be that only one woman a month would sell a kidney to a broker, but lately it has gotten a lot worse," Selvam says. "Now it's two women a week, and I know I have to do something."

While we talk a woman in a blue and highlighter-yellow sari frowns at him from across the courtyard. She looks like she is in her midforties, but I suspect that rough living in an Indian slum might mark her closer to thirty. The edge of a foot-long scar crests across her exposed abdomen over the fold in her sari. Selvam tells me that just about every adult woman here has a scar like that. "I haven't been able to stop a thing," he says.

Weeks after the wave swept away his village, the government relocated the twenty-five hundred residents from their fertile fishing grounds to this worthless patch of land. The settlement is next to a giant power station that pumps electricity to Chennai, and yet power outages are still common here. The villagers' needs are modest: they want fishing nets and a small three-wheeled rickshaw so that the fishermen can haul the community's catch to market. Ever since they were relocated, Selvam has lobbied the high courts to send the cash and resources they promised.

His pleas fell on deaf ears until January 2007, when he had had enough. That was when he decided to play the only card he had left at a meeting scheduled to take place in front of one of Chennai's most powerful high-court justices.

The plan was simple enough. By using the testimony of poor women who were forced to sell their organs, the court would be shamed into finally administering aid. After all, how could the court *not* empathize with his village's plight once it learned about the level of desperation fostered by government inaction.

In a crowded community hall the judiciary listened to Selvam's breathless testimony and the stream of courageous women who volunteered their stories. They said that kidney brokers had always been a problem—even before the tsunami—but now they were relentless. They showed their scars and Selvam waited eagerly for the judge to open up the state's coffers.

Things didn't go according to plan. The judge listened carefully, but the aid was tied up in India's obscene bureaucracy, not because of a lack of judicial will. To make matters worse, the five hundred men and women in the audience nearly rioted when they realized that Selvam had betrayed their secret. Showing the women's scars shamed the entire village. Everyone knew that they were poor, but being poor enough to sell organs was another thing. Youths shouted that he had dishonored the women of his community by exposing what they felt should have been a private matter.

The revelation didn't push the government into sending the camp the nets and vehicles he requested. All it did was expose the village's dirty secret to the press. Local newspapers began covering the scandal, and soon the state's Department of Medical Services uncovered evidence that fifty-two Indian hospitals were involved in what amounted to one of the country's largest coordinated organ thefts ever.

Even though Selvam had failed in his goal, the investigation was an opportunity to turn the tide against the practice of kidney selling and bring brokers and corruptible health officials to task. Public outcry against the scandal forced the state-level ministers to form an offical response.

The job fell to Tamil Nadu's health minister, K. K. S. S. R. Ramachandran.* A former political party street tough who is known by the impenetrable string of initials in front of his name, he earned his stripes with the government after a political rival threw a jar of acid in his face. (The scars make him noticeable at party meetings.) To the surprise of locals he forwent police action. Rather than try the issue in the courts, he planned to resolve it through mediation. He gathered the state's top transplant doctors in a room in a spur-of-the-moment conference and made them swear to stop selling organs and try to use more cadavers instead.

---

* In South India names are often preceded by strings of initials. While there is no family name as there is in the West, the initials often indicate where someone was born and their father's name and religious affiliation. In accordance with the custom, I have only listed the initials throughout the book.

Resolved to let the doctors police themselves, he let the community off with only a token slap on the wrist.

But he had to make some concessions to a public that was out for blood. To show that he was tough on crime, the ministry closed two of the smallest and most ill equipped nursing homes that were tangentially linked to illegal transplants. The rest of the city's transplant teams breathed a sigh of relief. Even though clear paper trails linked dozens of surgeons to the previous year's more than two thousand illegal kidney transplants, within a few months Chennai was back to business as usual.

For Selvam and thousands of other poor Tamilians who never got their equal share of India's rising fortunes, selling organs still sometimes feels like their only option in hard times.

"In other parts of India people say that they are going to Malaysia or the United States with a glimmer of hope in their eyes. In Tsunami Nagar people speak that way about selling their kidneys," he tells me.

Tsunami Nagar is far from unique. The ample supply of available organs in the third world and excruciating long waiting lists in the first world make organ brokering a profitable occupation. Not only has demand for kidneys risen steadily over the last forty years, but poor people around the world often view their organs as a critical social safety net.

Since the inception of antirejection drugs like cyclosporine, international cabals of doctors and corruptible ethics boards have slowly transformed slums in Egypt, South Africa, Brazil, and the Philippines into veritable organ farms. The dirty secret of the organ business is that there is no shortage of willing sellers.

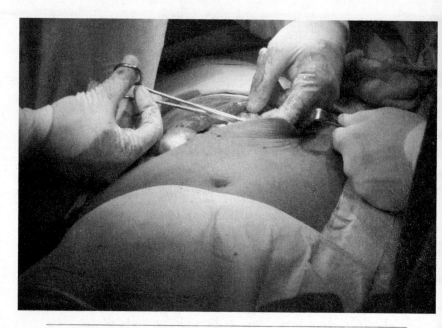

A nephrectomy taking place at a hospital in Chennai, India. In 2006 and 2007 almost all of the women in a tsunami refugee camp nicknamed "Kidneyvakkam" sold their organs to a cabal of brokers and middlemen. Patients from India and abroad flock here to buy human organs at a discount and to escape long wait times in their home countries.

For someone living on less than a dollar a day, $800 is almost an unthinkably large sum of money. The payment offers an unfair incentive, coercion that pits abject poverty against a global capitalist enterprise.

If the organ shortage could be reduced to numbers and figured like an algebra problem, it would not be difficult to find living donors for the one hundred thousand people on the United States' organ transplant waiting list. Third world sellers are easy to find, and they offer a cost-effective solution to the problem. A transplant at an Indian hospital costs about one-twentieth of what it does in the United States.

The economic logic is so persuasive that several American insurance agencies want a piece of the action. Two of them, IndU-Shealth and United Group Programs, estimate that it is cheaper to cover the cost of a cheap kidney transplant abroad than paying for years of expensive, and ultimately lethal, dialysis treatments at home. These and other companies have relationships with hospitals in India, Pakistan, and Egypt that can arrange organ transplants almost on demand. Outsourcing plans like theirs were so persuasive that in February 2006 the West Virginia legislature considered a formal health-care plan for state employees that offered rebates to patients who chose to get their transplants done in a foreign hospital. By the time of publication the law was still pending, and yet little seems to have changed in the overall situation. (It should be noted that IndUShealth's website states that while the company will pay for the transplant, patients seeking live-donor tissue have to arrange for their own donor, something relatively easy to do with the right hospital contacts.) For recipients, the red market has a clinical leg up on the legal competition. Living-donor transplants are by and large more successful than cadaver donations. Patients who get kidneys from paid donors live longer than those who receive their organs from brain-dead patients.

Despite the cost and health benefits of live organs, there is simply no ethical justification to cross legal jurisdictions and buy tissue. Brokers can make purchasing an organ easy, but organ sellers don't talk about how selling organs changed their lives for the better.

Almost every woman in Tsunami Nagar has a story about how organ brokers took advantage of her during her most desperate hour. One woman, Rani, complains that since her operation even walking across the village's dirt road hurts so severely that she has to break it up into small, manageable steps.

Rani's troubles began when her husband lost his fishing job and took up drinking full-time. Perpetually without money Rani was unable to provide even a modest dowry when her daughter Jaya got married, and Jaya's mother-in-law and new husband took out their disappointment on Jaya. They forced her to do extra work, doled out beatings when they saw fit, and generally made her life as miserable as possible. Within a month, she came home to her mother, said good-bye, and then tried to take her own life by drinking a quart of pesticide.

When Rani found her daughter passed out on the small family cot, she gathered her up in her arms and carried her to a local hospital. Doctors there had seen their fair share of suicides-by-pesticide and had neutralizing agents ready. In a few hours they stabilized her, but she would have to remain in the intensive care ward for more than a week. Rani couldn't afford the extended hospital stay, and staff members said they would have to stop treatment without a payment guarantee. Rani had to come up with money quickly or, they told her, her daughter would die.

Over the years so many people had sold their kidneys in Tsunami Nagar that wry locals began calling the camp "Kidneyvakkam" or "Kidneyville." Brokering kidneys was a cottage industry, with women who already had sold their kidneys brokering sales for their friends. Brokers routinely quote a high payout—as much as $3,000 for the operation—but usually only dole out a fraction of the offered price once the person has gone through it. Everyone here knows that it is a scam. Still the women reason that a rip-off is better than nothing at all.

One of Rani's friends had sold her kidney a year earlier and told her that a broker named Dhanalakshmi ran a tea shop outside of Devaki Hospital in Chennai as a front for her real business: proffering organs on the black market. Dhanalakshmi gave Rani $900 up front to cover her daughter's expenses and promised $2,600 more when the procedure was over. Dhanalakshmi made it clear that if Rani backed out, thugs on her payroll would sort out the situation with violence.

Before the transplant, Rani gave blood and urine to prove that she was a match for the buyer, who was a wealthy Muslim woman. When her blood work passed muster she was sent to the city's General Hospital to pass an ethics review by the Transplant Authorization Committee.

Responsible for ensuring that all transplants are legal and unpaid for, the committee is authorized to oversee and stop kidney rackets from forming in the first place. Despite its noble aims, the committee rarely lives up to its charter and routinely approves illegal transplants through brokers. Its members are meticulous about covering their tracks, and give the procedures every appearance of legality. As long as the committee hearings proceed along a mutually understood pantomime between organ sellers and buyers, the committee can say that it did everything it could to ensure the transaction was ethical. After all, everyone who appears before the committee is under oath to tell the truth. Rani's broker had coached her to speak only when spoken to, hand over a packet of forged papers, and then leave as quickly as possible. Rani said that

sometime before the meeting, Dhanalakshmi paid a ₹2,000 bribe
to be sure everything went smoothly.

Rani wasn't alone in the committee's waiting room; three
other women were there to sell their kidneys.

"We went up one at a time and all [the committee] did was
ask me if I was willing to donate my kidney and to sign a paper. It
was very quick," Rani said.

With the paperwork out of the way, she checked into Devaki
Hospital for the surgery. The procedure went according to plan,
but the recovery was more difficult than she had expected. Her
neighbor who helped arrange an introduction to Dhanalakshmi
sat by her bedside day and night. But after three days—with her
wound still draining liquid—the hospital sent her home. When
she went back to the hospital a week later for a checkup, the doctors pretended not to recognize her.

Meanwhile the broker predictably vanished during the time it
took Rani to recover, and she realized she'd been cheated.

Now the pain in her side prevents her from getting the only
work available: day labor on local construction sites. When I ask
her whether it was worth it, she says, "The brokers should be
stopped. My real problem is poverty—I shouldn't have to sell my
kidney to save my daughter's life."

In another case, Mallika, a thirty-three-year-old woman living a mile from Tsunami Nagar, says she made the decision to
sell an organ to try to move beyond her meager existence doing
laundry work. But the decision may have ended up costing the life
of her son. I meet her in her one-room hut on a street that smells
of rotting fish and open sewage. She is sweating profusely, which

is something she doesn't chalk up to Chennai's unbearable heat but rather to the poor follow-up care she received after doctors removed and sold her kidney.

Just a handful of days before the tsunami a broker named Rajji, who now runs a tea stall near the docks, said he could help her out with her cash problems.* His deal seemed straight-forward: $3,000 for her kidney with $750 up front. Even now the thought of the cash makes her smile. Within days she was issued paperwork with a false name and, like Rani, cleared the bureaucratic hurdles without a problem. Soon she was packed away to Madurai, a smaller city in Tamil Nadu where members of Rajji's network brought her to doctors at a branch of the inter-nationally known Apollo Hospital. They removed her kidney and transplanted it into a wealthy Sri Lankan transplant tour-ist, whose police records indicate that he paid $14,000 for the operation. The recuperation took longer than she had expected, and she wasn't able to return to Chennai for twenty days. The hospital refused to provide for her accommodation, and even the cost of postoperative drugs came out of her own pocket. When she returned to Chennai, Rajji said he wouldn't pay her even one more rupee.

After two years of begging for cash, she filed a police com-plaint. She alleged that she had been defrauded of her organ. But the police saw it a different way. When they arrested Rajji under

---

* In a coincidence that I have yet to understand, organ brokers across India often have a second business running tea stalls. Perhaps it is because stall owners tend to know many people who can afford little else than a ₹2 cup of chai and are easy targets for organ schemes.

charges of organ trading, they also threatened to arrest her for agreeing to sell her kidney.

"Both of them broke the law," says a plainclothes police investigator in the police headquarters. "If we prosecute one, we should also arrest the other." A week later Rajji was back on the streets with only a warning. When I track him down from an address on the police report, he is manning his small tea stall. He tells me that he is really the victim as he boils a cup of sugary Nescafé.

"I am just trying to help people. I learned that someone was dying with kidney failure. I also know that there are many people here willing to sell. What is the problem with that? This should be legal," he says. When I ask about the missing money, he denies ever offering Mallika more than $750. "I gave her only what it was worth." Besides, he says, he shared his cut of the sale with several other tiers of brokers and doctors, netting only about $300 for himself.

While Mallika says that she never fully recovered from the surgery, she also tells me that her teenage son, Kannan, has contracted hepatitis B, which is now causing his kidneys to shut down. "Soon he is going to need a transplant, and I won't have anything to give him," she says. Even if she could find a hospital willing to donate medical services to her son, she would never be able to find the cash to buy a kidney. Flesh in India moves up the social hierarchy, not down.

The brokers who negotiated with Rani and Mallika were on the lowest rung in a series of intermediaries, each of whom took a cut of the $14,000 price tag for the transplant. Rajji claims that his cut was just a fraction of the total, the bulk of the commission going to a high-volume organ dealer in Madurai named Shankar.

While Shankar has since vanished without a trace, the identities of the higher-level people in the business are an open secret. Just a mile from Tsunami Nagar is K. Karppiah, who is widely considered one of the most active players in the kidney trade. His name is spoken in hushed whispers. And over the course of a month, dozens of kidney sellers fingered him, saying that he gets a cut of every kidney sold. As a kingpin broker he rarely makes contact directly with patients or vendors, but is a middleman who makes the entire system function. When I showed up at his house, he declined to be interviewed. But even the man outside laying asphalt knew what a powerful player he was. "Everyone knows Karppiah," he said. "On this street, all the houses are his."

Without the lucky break of someone coming forward with his or her story and a subsequent police investigation, it is almost impossible for an outsider to follow the story of an organ's path as it travels from seller to buyer. Despite being housed at the same hospital, the patients who bought Rani's and Mallika's kidneys never introduced themselves to the sellers. The string of middlemen from Rajji, Dhanalakshmi, and Karppiah to the doctors who perform the operation keep the supply chain secret. After all, it's in the middlemen's best interest to never let the patient and seller negotiate directly. Secrecy is the key to maintaining the inflated fees they charge for a simple introduction.

While middlemen have a clear financial incentive to keep the specifics of the supply chain secret, hospitals and doctors use the sophisticated language of patients' rights to keep the entire process behind closed doors. Even in legitimate cadaver donations in the West, hospitals argue that disclosing the name of the donor to the recipient harms the privacy of everyone involved.

Of the six hospitals I visited on a list of more than fifty that the Indian government claimed were performing illegal kidney transplants in Chennai, surgeon after surgeon told me that donors and recipients would come to great psychological harm if they were ever allowed to meet each other.

BUT THAT HASN'T ALWAYS been the case. In her book *Strange Harvest,* about the cadaver donation system in the United States, anthropologist Leslie Sharp writes that anonymity between donors and recipients is a recent addition to medical ethics. In the 1950s, when transplants were first becoming popular in the United States, doctors argued that introducing donors' families to recipients would enhance the clinical success of the operation by allowing the two to share medical histories and perhaps even bond over the transplant. As the transplant industry grew more profitable, organs started to get stripped of their human history. Anonymity was the new norm.

But by the time Sharp began her research in the early 1990s, "transplant professionals regarded written communication, and even more so, personal communication [between donors and recipients] as subversive acts."* Clinical staff went so far as to diagnose donors searching for their organ history as pathological.

Sharp's research suggests that both donors and recipients generally want to know about each other, but are prevented by medical personnel. She writes that in public events where the

---

* Leslie Sharp, *Strange Harvest* (Berkeley: University of California Press, 2006), 166.

transplant community comes together, "tales of personal encounters always generate spontaneous responses of joy and celebration from the audience."* And yet hospitals routinely seal records and keep the two sides apart. Sharp uses the word *biosentimentality,* the way donors and recipient families want to know the history of an organ for a sense of continuity between two living beings, to describe the unique relations created by transplant technology. However, despite this yearning there is a much more practical reason to do away with the notion of medical privacy.

In the context of international organ sales even when patients know they are buying an organ, doctors use the privacy ethic to trump any suspicion of exploitation along the supply chain. And yet what is worse: exposing the stories of people who sell their tissue under duress, or allowing brokers free and unfettered control of the organ supply? There is a clear conflict of interest when doctors and brokers are able to play the role of both profit-taking middleman and health-care provider. With total control of the supply chain, anonymity provides the perfect cover for extortion and criminal activity.

Since the early 1990s academics and journalists have been aware of the neocannibalistic demand for transplantable organs. Nancy Scheper-Hughes, an anthropologist at the University of California–Berkeley, has spent the better part of the last two decades researching and exposing the hypocrisies of international organ networks. In 2000 her landmark article "The Global Traffic in Human Organs" investigated organs being mined from

---

* Ibid.

Brazilian favelas, South African shantytowns, Indian slums, and Chinese prisons, and through Iranian state-funded programs.

Her most profound insight, however, is not to catalog the scale of organ trafficking but to question our bedrock assumptions about the nature of organ scarcity in the first place. She equates the insatiable demand for organs to our medical hubris in the face of mortality. She says that medical mythology promises the "unprecedented possibility of extending life indefinitely with the organs of others." Transplant lists like the one perpetually updated by the United Network for Organ Sharing bloat as doctors tell dying patients that the only way to save their lives is to receive a functioning liver or kidney to replace the failing parts in their own bodies.

The reality is that while a transplanted organ is far preferable to being tethered to a dialysis machine or DeBakey heart pump, patients are merely trading a fatal disease for a chronic one. The new tissue often extends their lives for only a handful of additional years. Transplant programs frequently advertise that to sign up as an organ donor is to give a "gift of life" and that successful transplants are "miracles." They rarely mention that posttransplant living generally falls short of a phoenixlike rebirth. Instead, recipients live on heavy regimens of antirejection drugs that lower their immune system and make them ideal hosts for fatal opportunistic infections.

Noting the ease with which brokers are able to locate human tissue, Scheper-Hughes writes, "the real scarcity is not of organs, but transplant patients of sufficient means to pay for them." While it is very difficult to directly pay a person to sell a kidney in the United States, the transplant list creates a pressing sense of scarcity. It's true that without paid donors most organs come from a limited supply in the United States, where we harvest organs from brain-dead patients, relatives, occasional spontaneous donations, and organ-sharing schemes. This limited amount of available tissue drastically falls short of demand and drives up the cost of transplants. The high prices support an entirely self-sufficient medical economy that involves special life-support suppliers, organ transporters, legal departments, doctors, nurses, social workers, and administrators who all have a financial stake in keeping the transplant business churning.

Since doctors and medical staff control how many people get admitted to the organ transplant list, they are able to inflate the overall eligibility for organ transplants and set a standard rate of available organs against the total supply. Oil cartels employ the same tactics. Over the years the number of available organs from donors has expanded greatly in America, and yet the ratio between donors and listees has remained more or less the same.

The transplant list—or more specifically the organ-harvesting network—creates an impression of scarcity that supports big-money medical centers. Patients with organ failure are told that their only hope is to get a replacement organ. The truth is more likely that patients will regain only a shadow of their lost health with the transplant. This is not to say that a more ethical organ system would rely on paid living donors. Instead, doctors and patients should think more realistically about mortality.

In America, however, it is taboo to suggest US transplant centers are in the business of buying and selling organs. They're here to save lives. Doctors are supposed to be above the humdrum world of commerce. And yet hospitals with transplant centers have a lot to gain financially. A transplant center is a sort of badge of quality that drums up business for all of a hospital's departments. Indeed, it is common for hospitals to advertise their transplant centers on highway billboards—not because many drivers are likely to need fresh organs, but to give the impression of overall excellence in all fields.

The National Organ Transplant Act outlaws buying and selling human tissue, but says nothing about the corollary services that surround organ transplants. Transplant surgeons and activists are quick to note that their centers do not actually sell organs, only transplant services. Those services can be pricey. In 2008 actuaries at Milliman calculated the total costs of different organ transplants in real terms. Including the total costs of procurement ($67,500 paid to the hospital to harvest a kidney), pre- and postoperative care, immunosuppressants, and hospital administration, a kidney transplant costs $259,000. Livers go for $523,400; pancreases, for $275,000; and intestines for a whopping $1.2 million. People don't go to a transplant center to buy medical services: They go to buy organs. In many cases only the wealthy or superinsured (and in some cases government-insured) can even consider the option. And an accounting trick does not change the facts.

The tremendous cost of not officially buying an organ coupled with an exceptionally long waiting list drives people abroad to centers that offer speedy and cheap services. The lower costs mean that people priced out of the American market for organs can find an affordable transplant solution abroad. And they don't even have to sacrifice quality. One of the places they go to is Aadil Hospital in Lahore, Pakistan, which advertises that the International Organization for Standardization rates it on a par with any hospital in the West.

These days, Aadil openly advertises two packages for transplant patients: $14,000 for the first transplant, $16,000 for people who need a second organ after the first has failed. "You do not have to worry about the donor. We shall provide a live donor arranged through a humanitarian organization, which has hundreds," said Abdul Waheed Sheikh, CEO of Aadil Hospital in an e-mail.

In India, Brazil, Pakistan, and China, hospitals advertise their surplus of willing donors to high-paying patients. The disparity in price between the first and third worlds is an opportunity for international brokers to extract obscene profits from patients who don't know how to book transplants on their own.

The price of a kidney transplant at one of the best hospitals in the Philippines, where organ sales are more or less legal, was just $6,316, according to a 2005 report by the Philippine Information Agency. The organ brokers who arrange transplants charge whatever they can and pocket the difference for themselves.

The incoming patient perceives the apparent supply shortage, but because of the power of international exchange they still get an organ for less than half the inflated US price. At the same time, legal confusion, fear, and an information gap have created a classic arbitrage scenario for connected vendors. The vast profits available to the middlemen have dented reform efforts.

Falling prices hit the lowest end of the chain hardest. As we have seen in Indian tsunami refugee camps, sellers work through organ brokers, who, assuming they pay at all, on average pay only a few thousand dollars for a healthy kidney. And that's despite booming demand. The World Health Organization in 2002 pegged the global number of people suffering from diabetes—a leading cause of kidney failure—at 171 million. By 2030 the number will have climbed to more than 366 million.

"Each country and each region therein has completely different situations than the next one," explains a Los Angeles–based organ finder doing business online at the website liver4you.org. He asks to be identified only as Mitch. "Since most overseas transplants are doctor-controlled, like [from] private medical practice in the United States, there is a wide range in prices. . . . The donors are in such huge supply where it's legal, like the Philippines, so they have to accept the average of $3,000 [for selling their kidneys]."

Savings are rarely passed on to the buyer. Their value inflates quickly once the organs move from the streets into the medical supply chain. Mitch says he typically charges between $35,000 and $85,000 for kidney transplants. Depending on where those operations take place, Mitch can clear $25,000 or more per transaction.

While players like Mitch capitalize on legal differences between countries, the practice of organ brokering seems to be ingrained in the very nature of transplants. And it fosters the general lack of transparency. Brokers play key roles keeping the process undercover while maximizing profit along the entire supply chain from the donor's body to the recipient's.

Some academics and economists contend that only a legal and regulated system can stop exploitation along the organ supply chain. They contend that paid donations will persist regardless of how the legal system is set up. Transplant surgeons like K. C. Reddy, one of the doctors involved in the Chennai scandal, say that such a system would allow for free movement of organs to needy patients while protecting the interests of the donors. It would guarantee the donors both excellent follow-up care and fair payment.

The free-market solution is seductive. It speaks to a belief in personal liberty and an inherent right to decide our own fates. It also adds an economic incentive that cuts out speculation by middlemen. However, real-world success stories are hard to come by. The bioethicist Arthur Caplan wrote that market solutions to the kidney shortage put vendors at a disadvantage, saying that their "choice is imperiled by high compensation, not because the sellers are rendered irrational by the prospects of money, but [because] for those in need of money certain offers, no matter how degrading, are irresistible."* In other words, there's always someone willing to sell their body parts for less than they are worth.

Legalization proponents often tout Iran as an example of a state that legalized sales and now has an abundance of organs. In Iran organ sales are legal as long as they are regulated by a central state agency. Donors are paid for their sacrifice and looked after by doctors during their recuperation. In turn, there is practically no waiting list for a new kidney.

When I called up the anthropologist Nancy Scheper-Hughes to talk about their solution, she turned sour. "When Iran legalized live donations, they bought the argument that the short supply of kidneys was really only a marketing problem. But when the government took over responsibility for managing the black mar-

---

* Arthur Caplan, "Transplantation at Any Price?" *American Journal of Transplantation* 4, no. 12 (2004): 1933.

ket kidney trade, the so-called brokers and kidney hunters were rebranded 'transplant coordinators.' But they're still just thugs who troll the streets and homeless shelters for people to donate on the cheap."

In other words, legalization didn't change the motivations of the people in the business, only legitimized their illicit tactics. The situation is even worse in China, where the state assumes total control of the organ market. Since 1984 China has harvested organs from prisoners on death row. In 2006 David Matas, a UN delegate, and David Kilgour, a retired member of Canada's Parliament, released *Bloody Harvest: A Report into Allegations of Organ Harvesting of Falun Gong Practitioners in China*. In it they interviewed dozens of former political prisoners, transplant hospital administrators, and people who had direct knowledge of post-execution organ harvesting. It's riveting if disturbing reading.

Between 2000 and 2005, they state, there were 60,000 officially recorded kidney transplants in China; of those, 18,500 came from identifiable sources that could be tracked to specific individuals and events. The remaining 41,500 were unaccounted for. Kilgour and Matas believe that many were harvested from Falun Gong religious practitioners—who were declared political dissidents in the late 1990s. Over the years thousands of practitioners have gone missing in Chinese prisons.

One of their sources, who used the pseudonym Annie, was the ex-wife of a transplant surgeon who performed more than two thousand cornea harvestings from living prisoners. Over the years he told her about the day-to-day goings-on at what can only be called an organ factory. She described underground networks of holding cells at Sujiatun Hospital that housed at least five thousand prisoners in pens. Doctors there fed the prisoners only meager rations. Every day doctors removed three prisoners from their cells.

She says that the captives were then "injected with a shot that caused heart failure. During the process they would be pushed into operation rooms to have their organs removed. On the surface the heart stopped beating, but the brain was still functioning because of that shot." Her husband would then receive the patients and quickly slice out the corneas and send the patient on a gurney down the hall where "their organs were removed while alive, and that it was not just cornea removals—they were removing many organs."

People have critiqued the Matas and Kilgour report for possible discrepancies in Annie's testimony, as well as the possibility that the execution spree may not have been levied only against the Falun Gong. And yet Falun Gong message boards contain a virtual tidal wave of photos of executed prisoners and bodies emptied of organs that are continually leaked out of China through surreptitious means.

Harry Wu, one of the foremost activists against human rights abuses in China and founder of the Laogai Research Foundation in Washington, DC, says that he interviewed a transplant surgeon who removed both kidneys from an anesthetized prisoner during a late-night surgery. The next morning the surgeon learned that the guards later shot the prisoner in the head.

In another case, plastic surgeon Guoqi Wang testified in front of the US House of Representatives in 2001 that he had harvested skin from prisoners while another transplant team of surgeons harvested internal organs. He claimed to be present at more than one hundred such operations between 1990 and 1995.

The prisoners had been executed with either bullets to the head or shots of heparin.

"Then, after the execution, the body would be rushed to the autopsy room, rather than the crematorium, and we would extract skin, kidneys, livers, bones, and corneas for research and experimental purposes. The skin was subsequently sold to burn victims for $1.20 per square centimeter." Sometimes, he said in front of Congress, the prisoners were still alive during the procedure, and writhing in agony after their organs had been removed. The government paid Wang a modest sum in cash ($24–$60) for each successful harvest.

Until recently it was easy for Americans to get kidneys from executed prisoners. In 2006 the website for the China International Transplantation Network Assistance, a government-sponsored body, advertised a straightforward price list: kidney, $62,000; liver, $98,000–$130,000; lung, $150,000–$170,000; heart, $130,000–$160,000; cornea, $30,000. The organs averaged one-fifth the price of an American cadaver organ—and a match could be made with as little as two weeks' notice.

Kilgour and Matas argue that the short wait time clearly indicates that there is a prison system–wide catalog of tissue type. They believe that when a customer orders a kidney doctors are able to search the catalog for as close a match as possible and then schedule the execution on demand. From the recipient's perspective this would provide the best possible clinical outcome—a perfect match from a living donor. However, the price of the transplant for the donor is death.

.   .   .   .

TO VERIFY THE EXISTENCE of such a catalog I traveled to Flushing, Queens, a thriving Chinese community a few miles outside of Manhattan. Main Street is a collage of cramped billboards full of Chinese characters and restaurant windows hung thickly with glazed ducks. Boxy concrete buildings recall the uninspired but durable architecture of East Asia. Here English is a distant second language to Mandarin.

In the late 1990s the Chinese government calculated that the total membership of Falun Gong exceeded the membership of its own Communist party and deemed the spiritual organization a threat. While most of the practitioners are content to simply practice their spiritual exercises, which resemble tai chi routines, it is one of the few groups to actively resist the Chinese government's injunctions. In one notable incident in 2002, members of the group raided and took control of nine television stations as well as a satellite uplink during the World Cup finals. During the hijacking they broadcast their own antigovernment propaganda. Sensing that Falun Gong could be a major political threat, the government cracked down. Hard.

Saturating the state media with accusations that the group practiced black magic and brainwashed its membership, the government banned the group from organizing in both public and private. There were steep penalties for violation. Starting in 1999 the central committee devised a cunning plan for their arrest.

In July 1999 thousands of Falun Gong practitioners registered their protest against the government ban at the Central Petition Bureau, giving their names and addresses along with their concern over their loss of human rights. Hua Chen, who goes by the name Crystal in America, was one of the first to register in Beijing. Just minutes after leaving the government office uniformed police officers cuffed her.

I meet her, ten years after her arrest, in a cramped office of a small Chinese publication that doubles as an activist hangout. Her English is perfect, due to years acting as a translator for a major American firm in Beijing. She looks considerably younger than her age and story of hardship would make me believe. She attributes her health to the daily exercises that comprise the bulk of Falun Gong doctrine.

She was sentenced without a trial to a forced labor camp and routinely handcuffed and beaten by guards who accused her of conspiring to overthrow the government. They released her after a few weeks, but she was arrested again in April 2000 when it was deemed that she had not learned her lesson. This time it would be six months of torture.

"The worst was when the guards put a tube down my throat and forced me to drink a liter of high-density salt water," she says to me calmly. "They were doing the same thing to other prisoners, but only the ones who were Falun Gong. The drug addicts and thieves were treated much better than we were. They thought that a drug dealer could be reformed, but not a Falun Gong." The liquid almost immediately sent her into shock as the salt diffused into her body. Later she learned that her cellmate died of the same procedure.

Every few months a doctor at the Gwong Detention Center would summon the three hundred Falun Gong prisoners at the clinic for a checkup. "They would take a vial of blood from each of us then send us back to our cells. The other prisoners were jealous that we were getting medical treatment, but they never gave us medicine. Only took our blood." It wasn't until years later that Crystal surmised they were logging her blood into a database for potential harvesting.

She said it was routine for prisoners to be transferred from one detention center to another, so she was never sure who was being executed, who was being set free, and who was just being transferred. "We had no idea what was going on. It was terrifying," she says.

No one is saying the Chinese government went after the Falun Gong specifically for their organs, but it seems to have been a remarkably convenient and profitable way to dispose of them. Dangerous political dissidents were executed while their organs created a comfortable revenue stream for hospitals and surgeons, and presumably many important Chinese officials received organs.

In recent years kidney transplants in China have tallied almost half a billion dollars in revenue. Much of that money has been coming in as dollars from foreign sources.

Thomas Diflo, director of renal transplantation at New York University's Medical Center, has long sympathized with the fates of his patients on the transplant list. For years he has sat helplessly as many of them died before they were eligible for a donor organ. But starting in the late 1990s some of his patients who had been stuck on dialysis appeared in his office with brand-new transplant kidneys. Under normal circumstances he would have been aware of any transplants performed in his jurisdiction. Eventually, some of them confided that they had bought donor organs from hospitals that said they used organs from executed Chinese prisoners. The operations had cost as little as $10,000.

When I asked him about his patients' rationalization for buying organs he wrote to me, "The patients were not bothered by the source of their organs. They had a pragmatic 'This guy's going to die, I can be cured of renal failure' approach." However, they still needed his postoperative care once they returned to the United States, and he wasn't sure if it was ethical for him to treat patients who had gone outside the system.

His quandary took him to his hospital's ethics committee and eventually to testify in front of Congress in 2001 along with Guoqi Wang, the plastic surgeon who had harvested skin from living prisoners. With the international pressure on China, the number of foreign kidney-transplant patients seeking organs from prisoners has declined. However, it is unlikely that the domestic market has changed at all.

"As the number of executions across China appears to be shrinking somewhat, the number of organ transplants seems to be increasing, the number of Falun Gong victims would thus appear to be growing. Foreigners are no longer getting the organs—no doubt because of all the bad PR the regime has received—and it is wealthy Chinese nationals who presumably are the beneficiaries of the new organ order," wrote David Kilgour in an e-mail.

Kidneys have long been the mascot for organ transplantation. Every human is born with two, but can survive perfectly well with one. When kidneys fail, they generally fail together. Despite their seeming spareness, the organ is not an unproblematic commodity. Organ harvesting industries exploit the bodies of disadvantaged people around the world. In profit-driven markets the poor are exploited and alienated from their flesh; in government-run programs the state takes control of human bodies and erases any illusion of free will.

Like all red markets the trade in internal living organs desperately lacks transparency along the supply chain. In India and Iran (not to mention Egypt, Brazil, and South Africa) brokers manipulate the price of organs so that consenting sellers get the least possible profit for their tissue and sell only in the most desperate situations. In China, identities of organ sources are shrouded in secrecy, but evidence of the secret detention camps and on-demand executions has managed to filter out. If true, it makes buying an organ there tantamount to supporting a revival of the Holocaust. And in the United States the transplant list is so slow, the operation so expensive, and kidney transplants marketed as so necessary that many people feel they have no option but to travel abroad to illicit markets.

While solutions to the overall problem will be complex and nuanced, any plan must include a heavy dose of radical transparency. As we shall see with international adoptions, privacy regulations allow criminal organizations to flourish. Simply opening all records and letting anyone inspect the sources of organs could radically change all organ politics. Since only hospitals can perform the operations, it should be easy to regulate the transaction. Though they would still exist, brokers and middlemen would have less leeway to take advantage of desperate people. China would have to publicly admit crimes against humanity to sell human tissue, and US hospitals that are in the business of buying and selling human body parts would have to be open about where they get their tissue in the first place.

The playground outside Malaysian Social Services (MSS), an orphanage implicated in more than one hundred cases of kidnapping for profit. Though the orphanage ceased its international adoption program in 1998, the police in Chennai, India, are still trying to locate the whereabouts of the missing children. The police say that MSS reaped several hundred thousand dollars in illicit profit for kidnapping children and selling them into the adoption stream.

CHAPTER FOUR
MEET THE PARENTS

A<small>FTER HOURS HUNCHED</small> behind the wheel of a rented Kia, flying past cornfields and small-town churches, I'm parked on a Midwestern American street, trying not to look conspicuous. Across the way, a preteen boy dressed in silver athletic shorts and a football T-shirt plays with a stick in his front yard. My heart thumps painfully. I wonder if I'm ready to change his life forever.

I've been preparing for this moment for months back in my home in Chennai, India, talking to khaki-clad officers in dusty police stations and combing through endless stacks of court documents. The amassed evidence tells a heartrending tale of children kidnapped from Indian slums, sold to orphanages, and funneled into the global adoption stream. I've zeroed in on one case in particular, in which police insist they've tracked a specific stolen child in India to a specific address in the United States. Two days ago, the boy's parents asked me to deliver a message to the American family via their lawyer, seeking friendship and communication. But after traveling across ten time zones to get here, I'm at a loss for how to proceed.

The dog-eared beige folder on the passenger seat contains the evidence—a packet of photos, police reports, hair samples, and legal documents detailing a case that has languished in the Indian courts for a decade. There's a good chance that nobody in this suburban household has a clue. I wait until the boy ambles around to the back of the house, then jog over and ring the bell.

An adolescent Indian girl with a curious smile answers the door. "Is your mother home?" I stammer. Moments later, a blond woman comes to the door in jeans and a sweatshirt. She eyes me suspiciously.

ON FEBRUARY 18, 1999, the day Sivagama last saw her son Subash, he was still small enough to balance on her hip. Sivagama—who, like many in the state of Tamil Nadu, has no last name—lives in Chennai's Pulianthope slum, a place about as distant from the American Midwest culturally as it is in miles. Children play cricket in bustling streets swathed in the unbearable humidity that drifts in from the nearby Indian Ocean. Despite the congestion, it's considered a safe area. Unattended kids are seldom far from a neighbor's watchful eye.

So when Sivagama left Subash by the neighborhood water pump a few dozen feet from their home, she figured someone would be watching him. And someone was. During her five-minute absence, Indian police say, a man likely dragged the toddler into a three-wheeled auto rickshaw. The next day, police believe, Subash was brought to an orphanage on the city's out-skirts that paid cash for healthy children.

It was every parent's worst nightmare. Sivagama and her husband, Nageshwar Rao, a construction painter, spent the next five years scouring southern India for Subash. The family never gave up hope that he was still out there alive. They employed friends and family as private detectives and followed up on rumors and false reports from as far north as Hyderabad, some 325 miles away. To finance the search, Nageshwar Rao sold two small huts he'd inherited from his parents and moved the family into a one-room concrete house with a thatched roof in the shadow of a mosque. The couple also pulled their daughter out of school to save money; the ordeal plunged the family from the cusp of lower-middle-class mobility into solid poverty. And none of it brought them any closer to Subash.

In 2005, though, there was a lucky break. A cop in Chennai heard reports of two men arguing loudly about kidnapping in a crowded bar. Under questioning, police say, the men and two female accomplices admitted they'd been snatching kids on behalf of an orphanage, Malaysian Social Services (MSS), which exported the children to unknowing families abroad. The kidnappers were paid ₹10,000, about $236 per child.

According to a police document filed in court, the orphanage's former gardener, G. P. Manoharan, specifically confessed to grabbing Subash; records seized from MSS show that it admitted a boy about the same age the next day—the same day Nageshwar Rao filed his missing-person report. He was adopted about two years later. The surrender deed, a necessary document that establishes that a mother can no longer care for her child and has relinquished claims on him to an orphanage, which I reviewed along with similar documents for other kids, is a fraud, police say: The conspirators changed the child's name to Ashraf and concocted a false history, including a statement from a fictitious birth mother.

From 1991 through 2003, according to documents filed by Chennai police, MSS arranged at least 165 international adoptions, mostly to the United States, the Netherlands, and Australia, earning some $250,000 in "fees."

Assuming the Indian police have their facts straight, the boy his parents seek has a new name and a new life. He most likely has no memory of his Indian mother or his native tongue. Most international adoptions are closed, meaning the birth parents have no guaranteed right to contact their child, and the confidentiality of the process makes it difficult to track kids who may have been adopted under false pretenses.

After Subash disappeared, Sivagama fell into a deep depression. Ten years later, she's still fragile, her eyes ringed by heavy dark circles. At the mention of her son's name, she breaks into tears, dabbing at the corners of her eyes with her sari.

"Why should we pay like this," she pleads, "for what criminals started?"

And why would a crowded orphanage conspire to steal children off the streets? Perhaps Subash was viewed as particularly adoptable due to his light skin and good health.

BACK IN CHENNAI, I hoped to learn more, and negotiated my tiny black Hyundai past an endless stream of lorries, rickshaws, and stray cattle toward the outskirts of the city, where MSS is located.

After the initial round of allegations, MSS closed the orphanage and no longer does international adoptions. However, it still runs several social programs and a school for young children.

I pulled up outside the bright pink building, got out, and peeked through the wrought-iron gate. A man in a crisp white shirt promptly intercepted me and then introduced himself as Dinesh Ravindranath, a name I recognized from police reports that list him as an accomplice in the kidnappings. He said he has been running MSS since his father died in 2006. He's also its lawyer.

Ravindranath told me that the investigation of his organization—which made headlines in India—has been blown out of proportion; he's the real victim here. The police, he alleged, have been using their investigation to extort money from the institution. "The law says that we cannot ask too much about the history of a woman who wants to give up her child to adoption, so we have to accept children on faith," he said.

But surrender deeds obtained during my search bear the signatures of MSS officials alongside those of the suspected kidnappers, who have admitted to handing over multiple children under different aliases. When I pressed Ravindranath about the fees the suspects told police they'd received from MSS, he claimed the situation was misconstrued. "We give the women two or three thousand rupees [about forty-seven dollars] when they come here out of charity, not as a fee for kidnapping," he said. "This happens everywhere. We are only the scapegoats."

The problems with adoption are certainly widespread. Over the past decade, scandals in Delhi and the Indian states of Gujarat, Andhra Pradesh, Maharashtra, and Tamil Nadu have exposed severe breaches of adoption protocol and claims by parents who have lost children to foreign families. The promise of lucrative adoption fees motivates orphanages to create a steady supply of adoptable children. It costs about $14,000 to bring a child to the United States from India, not including the standard $3,500 fee to the orphanage. In the most egregious cases, once-respected agencies get wrapped up in child trafficking, and well-meaning American families never realize they're not adopting a child— they're buying one.

The scandals aren't limited to India. In 2007 employees at the French charity Zoe's Ark were arrested trying to fly out of Chad with 103 children they claimed were Sudanese war refugees; police later determined that most of the kids had been stolen from families in Chad. In China's Hunan province half a dozen orphanages were found to have purchased nearly one thousand children between 2002 and 2005, many of whom ended up in foreign homes. In the spring of 2008 an ABC News team discovered that some institutions in the region were still purchasing children openly for $300 to $350.

In 2006 celebrity watchers were riveted by Madonna's adoption, from a Malawi orphanage, of David Banda, a child who is not, in fact, an orphan. In January 2009 workers from the Utah adoption agency Focus on Children pleaded guilty to fraud and immigration violations; according to a federal indictment, they had imported at least thirty-seven Samoan children for adoption after misleading the birth parents and telling prospective adoptive parents that the kids had been orphaned or abandoned. After an earthquake turned much of Haiti into rubble, several members of an Idaho-based Christian church group were arrested trying to take children out of the country without permission.

"This is an industry to export children," says Sarah Crowe, UNICEF's media director for South Asia. "When adoption agencies focus first on profits and not child rights, they open up the door to gross abuses."

The Hague Convention on Intercountry Adoption, which addresses this type of criminal exploitation, was ratified by fifty countries—the United States signed on in 2007—but the pact is toothless, according to David Smolin, a law professor at Alabama's Samford University who has adopted two children from India. "The Hague itself has the weakness of relying on [the] sending countries to ensure that the child was properly relinquished," Smolin told me via e-mail. "Receiving countries cannot afford to simply take the sending country's word."

Smolin should know. His adopted kids were placed in orphanages in Andhra Pradesh by their birth mother to receive an education—a practice not uncommon among India's poor. But the illiterate mother was tricked into signing a surrender deed at the outset and was later turned away when she tried to regain custody. The girls, nine and eleven, had been coached to say their father was dead and their mother had given them up, but they eventually told the Smolins the truth. The American adoption agency refused to look into the matter. By the time the family tracked down the birth parents, six years had passed, and the girls had acclimated to life in Alabama. Although the kids remain here, the Smolins opened up the adoption; they have traveled to visit the Indian family and kept in regular contact.

Smolin has since retooled his legal career, and he is now among the nation's leading advocates of adoption reform. The Hague convention's biggest flaw, he notes, is that it doesn't cap the adoption fees paid by rich countries. "If you don't sharply limit the money, all of the other regulations are doomed to failure," Smolin says.

Police, lawyers, and adoption advocates in India echo this sentiment. "If you didn't have to pay for a child, then this would all disappear," says Deputy Superintendent S. Shankar, the lead investigator in Subash's case who requested that his full name not appear in print.

When the Chennai police first linked Subash to the United States based on MSS documents, they called Nageshwar Rao into the station to identify his son from a photo lineup. He quickly pointed to a snapshot police say they recovered from Ashraf's orphanage file that had been taken just days after he had been admitted. Subash was lying on a comfortable bed, dressed like a Western child, recalled Nageshwar Rao, as he reclined on a plastic deck chair in his cluttered abode flanked by Subash's teenage siblings Sasala and Lokesh. "Even after almost six years, I recognized him immediately," he says.

The police commissioner was satisfied with the identification, but told the father to forget his boy. Subash was better off in America. "The police treated me like I was nobody, but how can I be happy that my son was stolen from me?" asks Nageshwar Rao. "I don't want my son to live his life thinking that we abandoned him."

At least he knows what likely became of his child. Some three hundred MSS adoptions (foreign and domestic) have yet to be investigated; police probes at the local level seem to progress only in response to media attention. The overall MSS inquiry has moved at glacial speed as it has been batted from city to state to federal police jurisdictions, narrowing in scope with each handoff. It's now with India's Central Bureau of Investigation, which is under court order to pursue just three MSS-related cases in which stolen slum children allegedly went to adoptive families—in Australia, the Netherlands, and the United States. The latter is Subash's case.

Shankar, the agent in charge, concedes that his agency's investigation only scratches the surface of the problem. In reality a family who can't afford a lawyer to usher its child-kidnapping claim through the courts process will likely see the case go nowhere. "At this point, all we see are ten-year-old cases," says the burly, gray-haired cop. He says that other orphanages have arisen to replace MSS. "But I have no power to investigate," he adds. "My hands are tied."

It wasn't too difficult, though, to obtain the American family's address from the records of Chennai's High Court—it's listed on the legal document that makes the adoption official. When I tell Nageshwar Rao that I'll be traveling to the United States to make contact with the family, he touches my shoulder and eyes me intently. He was greatly relieved when the police told him his son was adopted, not trafficked into the sex trade or sold to organ brokers as he'd heard. Now he just wants some role in Subash's life. With the few words of English at his disposal, he struggles to convey his hopes. Gesturing into the air, toward America, he says, "Family." He then points back at himself. "Friends," he says.

TWO DAYS AND EIGHT thousand miles later, on a front stoop in the Midwest, I'm finding communication equally difficult. Clutching the evidence folder, I introduce myself, grasping for the right words. The boy has come back from behind the house to stand next to me; his sister is listening just inside the door. The teenager has Nageshwar Rao's same round face and fuzzy hair. I tell the mom we have to talk, but not in front of the kids. We agree to meet elsewhere after her husband gets home.

An hour later, in an empty park two blocks away, I lean against my rental car, checking my watch every other minute. Finally the father pulls up. He doesn't get out, but rolls down the window to talk. He seems unsurprised at what I have to say. "I saw something about this in the news a few years ago. I knew that it was a possibility," he says. "I've never been able to tell my son about it. It would be too traumatic." He flashes a nervous smile, and I hand him the folder. It includes the letter assuring that Subash's parents don't aim to reclaim the boy, but hope his new family will engage in friendly communication so that the Indian parents can still be part of his life. I ask the father to look the materials over, and we arrange to meet again the next day.

The American family didn't go through MSS directly. Like most, they used an agency. When I first wrote about Subash's case in *Mother Jones,* my editors and I agreed that we would withhold his name and other details in order to extend extra protections to the identity of the Midwestern family. At the time of publication I was only aware of one case involving the agency and gave it the benefit of the doubt that the suspicious adoption may have been random. After all, the American agency could have been easily duped by the orphanage that was sending it children.

A week after going to press the situation changed when I learned about a 1991 case involving Banu, an impoverished mother of three whose husband had died in an industrial accident. At the time, she was unable to care for her children, and lacking other options she accepted an offer from a school that said it would board and educate her children for free.

Seven years later, Banu, returned to the orphanage and asked the director K. Raghupati for her children back. Raghupati refused. He told her that she had relinquished custody and that he'd sent her kids to adoptive families in the United States. In Wisconsin, a local adoption agent named Ramani Jayakumar had worked with an agency called Pauquette Adoption Services to facilitate the children's transfer to America.

Banu filed a case in the Chennai High Court, and in 2005, the police arrested Raghupati on an assortment of charges related to adoption fraud. The adoption records were opened so that Banu could reconnect with her children, and in 2006, activists in America and India were able to introduce her to her now grown children.

Pauquette Adoption Services has arranged 1,441 international adoptions since 1982, including, according to court records, Subash's.

JUST INSIDE THE ENTRANCE to Pauquette's offices—a stately brick building opposite an elementary school—are bulletin boards overflowing with worn photos, kids it has placed from all around the world. I find the co-owner sitting behind the front desk. Lynn Toole, one of the owners, is not happy to make my acquaintance.

She concedes that she has followed the adoption scandals in the Indian press, but maintains that the Indian government signed off on every case her agency brokered. She'll cooperate with an investigation if need be, but won't discuss the case with me. When I ask her why she never contacted the family to warn them they may have adopted a kidnapped child, she refuses to comment. She hangs up when I make a follow-up phone call a week later. However, their website indicates that the agency continues to facilitate Indian adoptions, charging at least $12,000 to $15,000 for its services.

Pauquette has never been under investigation for anything involving international adoptions, says Therese Durkin, attorney for the Wisconsin Department of Children and Families that regulates Pauquette, nor was the department aware of any irregularities. Even when complaints do surface, the state has little investigative power. "All we have is the paperwork," Durkin says. "And we can only look at the face validity of the documentation." While adoptions from India require extensive recordkeeping, there's no way to know if a document is forged, she adds; communication between Indian and American authorities on this issue is practically nil.

In short, there's no way to know for sure where some of these children come from. During her ten-year tenure at a US agency now known as Families Thru International Adoption, Beth Peterson worked closely with some of the largest and most respected Indian orphanages, helping arrange American homes for more than 150 children. In the process, she came to believe that many orphanages have become de facto businesses that engage in criminal activity. That's unlikely to change so long as the financial incentive remains, says Peterson, who currently runs iChild, a support website for families adopting from India.

Prior to 2002, for instance, Peterson had sent upward of $150,000 to an Indian orphanage called Preet Mandir. The conditions were terrible—three babies died there while awaiting clearance for adoption by Peterson's clients. And when orphanage director, J. Bhasin, began illegally demanding thousands of dollars above and beyond the usual donation, and would not relinquish the children without the payments, Peterson severed the relationship. She later filed a complaint about Preet Mandir and its director with the Indian government.

Four years later, reporters from the Indian TV news network CNN-IBN approached Preet Mandir posing as adoptive parents, and Bhasin told them they could buy two children for $24,000. The resulting story led to revocation of the orphanage's adoption license, but the Indian government has since reinstated it on a probationary basis. "The profit motive exists on both sides," Peterson says. "One American agency I worked with just wanted to know that I could get them a certain number of babies a year, and wasn't concerned with where they came from."

In general, so long as the documents appear to be in order, US adoption agencies tend not to look much further. Children's Home Society & Family Services, one of America's largest agencies, arranged some six hundred international adoptions in 2007. David Pilgrim, vice president of adoption services, says he's confident that none of the children came from unethical sources. "We thoroughly vet all of the orphanages that we deal with, both in the past and in the present," he says.

However, Children's Home Society had worked with Preet Mandir up until the scandal broke. Asked whether any of these adoptions concerned him, Pilgrim pauses. "Our lawyers looked over the papers and didn't see any cause to worry," he says.

ONE DAY AFTER MY first encounter with the American couple, we're sitting together at a weathered picnic table in the cold park. A police cruiser slows down and the officer eyes us briefly before resuming down the street. Tears stream down the mother's cheeks. I can't tell whether she's furious or heartbroken. Maybe both. "To him, India does not exist," she says.

The couple tells me that the boy—whom they have given a new name—is their third adoption from India. Although this was the first time that they went through Pauquette, the process wasn't much different; they paid $15,000 in fees, and flew to India to see the orphanage and meet the owners of MSS. "We had the adoption bug," the husband explains. "Regulations change so much. We looked at Korea and South America, but India was the most open"—as in least difficult.

I've told the couple all I know about the Indian police's case—the alleged kidnapper's confessions, the child's age and timing of admission to the orphanage, the allegedly forged surrender deed, the father's photo identification, the legal document relinquishing Ashraf to their household. But they still aren't convinced. "We need to know more to believe it," the husband says. DNA evidence may be the only way to know for sure. But what do you tell the kid getting the blood test? And if it's negative, how can the family in India be sure the samples were properly collected?

An interim step would be for the two families to get in touch. But the American parents haven't decided where they stand. "We need to talk with our lawyer," the husband says with a frown. "We have to consider our son's best interest. What would it do to him if he found out?"

There's no road map for what comes next. As Nageshwar Rao discovered, there is little political will to pursue stolen children. With the passage of years, the ethical boundaries grow fuzzier still—although it's worth pondering whether any moral statute of limitations would be applied in the case of an American child kidnapped and raised in an Indian slum.

The Hague convention isn't much help. It neither lays out whether kidnapped children must be returned to their birth parents nor considers the impact of such a reunion on a child with no memory of those parents. René Hoksbergen, who studies adoption as a senior psychology professor at Utrecht University in the Netherlands, says the boy should hear the story—eventually. "The kidnapping issue could be told in different ways, but not now; the child is too young for this," Hoksbergen told me via e-mail. In the meantime, he says, the American parents should reach out to the Indian parents and send them news and photographs to help ease their grief. So long as all agree that it's the same child.

And that's where things get even messier. Back in Chennai, two months after our meeting in the park, I haven't heard a peep from the American couple. They ignore my follow-up e-mails, and Sivagama and her husband are distraught. "You met them, you tell me they are good people, and you saw our son, so why will they not speak to us?" Nageshwar Rao implores. "We know he is in a good home. It's not realistic for us to ask for him back, but let us at least know him."

He urges me to send the Americans another e-mail, this one describing several birthmarks and a small scar that weren't mentioned in the folder that I gave them. In the morning, I find a reply in my inbox. The adoptive father responds that his son has none of the marks Nageshwar Rao described. "At this point we are going to do nothing else," he concludes. "Please convey our condolences to the family. We do understand what they must be going through and what a blow this will be to them."

When I share this information with Deputy Superintendent Shankar, the cop is skeptical. "They could be lying, or maybe the birthmarks have disappeared," he muses. "We have no doubt that we have made a match; everything points in the direction of [the American family]."

Besides, he says, the matter may soon be settled once and for all—an Interpol request his agency made this past August seeking blood and hair samples from the boy has finally reached the US Attorney General's office. From there, it could get routed to the FBI for follow-up.

Even that is no guarantee. Should the couple decide to fight an FBI request, a good lawyer could likely tie up the matter until the child reaches adulthood—at which point any decisions in the matter would fall to the young man.

A YEAR AFTER THE initial investigation into Subash's identity the case has barely moved forward. The Indian police remain perpetually on the verge of filing another charge sheet, and yet never quite get there. The family in America remains silent. News of them has slowed to a trickle; only one anonymous comment on the *Mother Jones* website gives any inkling of what they are thinking. A commenter who claims to be close to the American family wrote:

> *It was the parents' decision not to disrupt the now stable life this child is experiencing based on the incomplete information from the family in India. When the child is older, the adoptive parents plan on telling him about the situation. If he wishes to pursue it, I know they will support him in his decision. All decisions of this family have been made, not for personal gratification, but out of genuine love for the mental well-being of their son. They are the closest to the situation. They know this child the best. Give them the freedom to make loving choices for their son based on all the information.*

A few months after that comment was posted, Shankar informed me that a DNA test was in the works. After years of pressure, the FBI collected samples and forwarded them to an Indian laboratory. From here it is a waiting game as the lab pushes through years of backlog until it eventually answers the question of Subash's identity scientifically.

The American family, however, has yet to make contact with Nageshwar Rao and Sivagama through any of the means available—with or without my involvement—to verify the police case independently. While claiming their child has no identifiable birthmarks, they have never allowed an outside party to verify dissimilarities.

But Nageshwar Rao remains hopeful. He continues with

his regular treks to an office building near the High Court, where he trades manual labor for representation by one of Chennai's top lawyers. He climbs the concrete steps to an office in the back, passing plate glass windows where legal clerks are filing hundreds of briefs, generating piles. Buried somewhere in this sea of paperwork are the petitions he has filed on behalf of his lost son.

Striding into the bustling office, he asks the first clerk he sees whether there has been any news from America.

Sivagama and Nageshwar Rao hold photos of their missing son Subash, who was kidnapped off the streets of Chennai in 1999. Police say that Subash now resides with a Christian family in the American Midwest. Although I was able to make contact with the American family, they have refused to confirm their child's identity, saying that when he reaches eighteen they will tell him that he may have been a victim of kidnapping.

Sub-zero storage containers designed to cryo-preserve human eggs. These buckets of eggs are in the basement laboratory of the Institut Marquès in Barcelona, Spain. Most people who sell their eggs in Spain are immigrants and students who earn between $800 and $1,500 for their donation.

CHAPTER FIVE
IMMACULATE
CONCEPTION

K RINOS TROKOUDES KNOWS this much about women: "If you pay something," he says, "you get lots of girls." Trokoudes does not mean that the way you may think. He is an embryologist. His business is harvesting human eggs. The thick mat of silver hair on his head matches the white lab coat that he wears every day, and his welcoming smile instantly sets his patients at ease as much as the medical diplomas that line his walls.

In 1992 he made the *Guinness Book of World Records* for facilitating a forty-nine-year-old woman to become pregnant through in vitro fertilization (IVF). The record has been broken several times over (by 2008 a seventy-year-old Indian woman gave birth to IVF-conceived twins), but Trokoudes' pathbreaking work helped cement his homeland of Cyprus's reputation as a place willing to push the boundaries in the field of embryology. Since then, through the quirks of geography, regulatory neglect, and global economics, the small island nation in the middle of the Mediterranean has become a focal point in the global trade in human eggs.

In one sense, a woman's ovaries hold the potential to bring life into the world, but they are also a gold mine of almost three million eggs just waiting to be harvested and sold to the highest bidder. Trokoudes sees it both ways. Since he started the Pedieos clinic in 1981, he has been working with a virtually unlimited supply of egg donors—mostly nonnative Cypriots who are relatively poor and find the cash they receive for donating eggs is an important supplement to their incomes. With a shrug of his shoulders he says, "Donors are available in areas where the income is low." Cyprus, which has both the inflated costs of an island nation and a large, poorly paid immigrant population, is the perfect incubator for cash-starved donors.

A full-service egg implantation with in vitro fertilization costs between $8,000 and $14,000 in Cyprus, about 30 percent less than the next cheapest spot in the Western world. Even more important, patients rarely have to wait more than two weeks to implant donor eggs, which is a blessing for people coming in from the United Kingdom, where strict limits on who can donate eggs have made the waiting list more than two years long. This year a third of his patients flew in from abroad and he hopes to double that number in the future.

"If you have the donors," he says, "you have everything."

Over the past decade the global demand for human eggs has grown exponentially and without clear guidelines, proliferating in lockstep with a fertility industry that has become a multibillion-dollar behemoth. Three decades after the introduction of in vitro fertilization, some 250,000 test-tube babies are born each year.

While the vast majority are still products of their biological mother's eggs, the desire of older, sometimes postmenopausal, women to become moms has fed the rapid growth of a questionably legal market for human eggs. The business now reaches from Asia to America, from the richest areas of London and Barcelona to backwaters in Russia, Cyprus, and Latin America.

The business features well-meaning doctors alongside assembly-line charlatans, desperate parents, and unlikely entrepreneurs, all competing for one source of raw materials: women of childbearing age. It is unevenly regulated, when it is regulated at all. While every country has attempted to control the domestic market, cheap airfare and loose international guidelines make dangerous and unethical sourcing as simple as obtaining a passport. Today poor women from even poorer countries sell their eggs to entrepreneurial doctors, who then sell them to hopeful recipients from rich countries. This has given rise to a spectacular set of ethical issues: Is it really okay to treat a woman like a hen, pumping her up with steroids so that we can farm her eggs for sale? Do the standards we apply to produce ball bearings also apply to the genetic building blocks of life and the women who bear them? Is the human egg a widget and the donor nothing more than a cog?

Unfortunately, nearly the entire Western world has punted on the ethical dilemmas. Some countries, like Israel, prohibit egg harvesting on its own territories, yet still reimburse citizens for IVF, even if it's done with donor eggs acquired in a foreign country.

US law says nothing about egg donation, although the American Society of Reproductive Medicine has nonbinding guidelines that deem any payment beyond reimbursement for lost wages and travel unethical. In Cyprus, as in the rest of the European Union, "compensation is allowed, but payment is not," says Cypriot health ministry official Carolina Stylianou, who is responsible for regulating the island's fertility clinics. Yes, that is as murky as it sounds.

All this mystery has helped create a vibrant marketplace with a wide range of prices and available services. In the United States, an egg implantation complete with a donor egg, lab work, and the IVF procedure itself runs upward of $40,000. The savings in Cyprus is incentive enough to bring people here from all over the world. For egg sellers (or donors, if you prefer) the price is truly all over the map. An American woman gets an average of $8,000 per batch of eggs, but can ask upward of $50,000 if she's an Ivy League grad with an athletic build. In the United States, where the market is the most open and prospective donors post their profiles online for patients to peruse, a one-hundred-point increase in SAT scores correlates with about a $2,350 rise in egg price. On the other hand, an uneducated Ukrainian who is doped with the preparatory hormones in Kiev and then flown to Cyprus for extraction and sent home without aftercare will get only a few hundred dollars for her batch of eggs.

The businesses, run like any other global industry, take advantage of differing legal jurisdictions as well as differences in income, local ethics, and standards of living to gain a competitive edge. According to the European Society of Human Reproduction and Embryology (ESHRE), every year more than twenty-five thousand people in Europe travel across borders for fertility treatments. While in principle a commercial market for human eggs could function ethically, the current international system targets specific populations of vulnerable potential egg donors and effectively creates two classes of people: those who sell flesh and those who receive it.

Unlike giving blood, donating an egg is a long and painful procedure that takes a minimum two weeks of hormone stimulation and then surgical removal. Like selling a kidney, it is not something that people choose to do lightly. They take on the risk of general surgery and anesthesia, as well as complications from the hormone injections that can be painful and sometimes fatal. Even so, the procedure has been wildly popular around the world, and increasing demand for eggs far outstrips the supply of altruistic individuals who are willing to donate their eggs for free to strangers solely out of the goodness of their heart.

However, the prevailing medical ethics around egg donation deem altruistic donation the only acceptable standard. This puts regulators in an untenable position. On the one hand, authorities in Europe and the United States need a large stable of donors in order to encourage the fertility business to grow and prosper. On the other hand, they want that business to be built around an altruistic system that limits the types of incentives that might make people willing to donate their eggs.

In terms of what motivates a person to give up her eggs, there isn't much difference between the words *compensation* and *payment* except that one translates to a lower price. Not surprisingly, these low payments only act as incentives for the poorest or most desperate people. Despite their good intentions, regulators have effectively given fertility clinics a subsidy for acquiring raw materials and allowed businesses to boom off the backs—and out of the wombs—of the poor. The relationship is almost never reciprocal.

Dr. Krinos Trokoudes, in Nicosia, Cyprus, runs a successful fertility clinic that attracts clients from abroad for egg implantation. Other clinics in Cyprus fly egg donors in from Ukraine and Russia for the express purpose of harvesting their genetic material. Egg sellers earn approximately $1,000–$1,500 for their time and trouble.

Cyprus, a recent member of the European Union, stands at the crux between taming its local market for human eggs with increased regulation that will lower supply, or liberalizing the trade and throwing open the door to payments and a large donor pool. In a way the island nation is a litmus test for the future of the flesh business. Already clinics in non–European Union countries like Russia and Ukraine are advertising their more-or-less unregulated egg business on the international market, but without the EU brand, few people want to travel there for fertility treatments. Even farther afield in countries like India, there doesn't seem to be any problem recruiting donors with cash. Cyprus offers the perfect business platform of a Wild West egg bonanza along with a reputation for administering top-quality medicine (and white babies).

Cyprus has more fertility clinics per capita than any other country, making it one of the most highly egg-harvested locations on the planet. Whether licensed or unlicensed, they offer IVF as well as a range of fertility services, even some that are typically proscribed elsewhere, like sex selection. The fertility business here blends the shady netherworld of gray market financial transactions with commercialization of human tissue. People travel here from Israel, from Europe, from all over the world. Couples who want a child can find cut-rate help here; while poor women find a market for their eggs. Cyprus is an egg bazaar that capitalizes on both sides of the supply-and-demand equation. Internationalization has made oversight laughable.

"The most aggressive reproductive clinics are run by shady people who operate in the full sun. They laugh at the idea that the world association or one of the national associations would revoke their membership. Regulators are dogs with no teeth. County and state medical societies and boards are only interested in these issues when they smack of abortion politics. At the international level, the specter of Cyprus, of all places, taking this role is incredibly problematic. . . . Cyprus is no more prepared to be a carefully run reproductive center than South Korea was poised to do human embryonic stem cell research," writes Glenn McGee, editor in chief of the *American Journal of Bioethics,* in an e-mail.

Cypriot surgeons like Dr. Trokoudes have been willing to push the boundaries of medicine from the moment they started their clinics. And sometimes they push too far. Consider the grandly named International IVF&PGD Centre, which has been the subject of numerous exposés and police investigations. The clinic was founded in 1996 as a go-to destination for Israelis seeking fertility treatment after paid egg donation was banned domestically. Known locally as the Petra Clinic, it can be found on a little-used coastal road between the fishing villages of Zygi and Maroni. On blustery winter days, when steady gusts of cold, salty wind barrage the dilapidated compound, it does not seem like an auspicious place to start life.

The day before, I spoke by phone with Oleg Verlinsky, son of the late owner, Yuri Verlinsky, who founded the Petra Clinic as a subsidiary of the Chicago-based Reproductive Genetics Institute. Yuri died in 2009 and the estate is still tied up in probate, but for now at least, Oleg runs the operation that also includes branches in Turkey, Russia, the Caribbean, and across the United States. In a hurried phone call he informed me that Petra is not primarily a fertility clinic—but it performs fertility-related services, including egg donation. He told me that it would be impossible for me to visit the clinic, which he said is used almost exclusively to treat rare blood disorders.

That surprised me. The clinic's website told a different story. In early February 2010, for example, it listed a menu of egg donors including a raft of Russians and Ukrainians. With stays as short as two or three days on the clinic's site, they receive their hormone doses at foreign clinics, the eggs are surgically extracted in Cyprus, and then they are flown home. There were no photographs, but the menu offered detailed descriptions. One entry read:

No. 17P, Ukrainian, Height 175, Weight 59, Blood type B+, Hair color: chestnut, Eye color: brown, Education:

University, Profession: artist, Age: 23, Date of arrival: Feb 2
10, Estimated aspiration date: Feb 05–07.

While fertility tourism has traditionally meant flying patients
to cheaper locations for budget treatment, Reproductive Genetics
uses Cyprus as a convenient transit point and exploits it as a legal
gray area for foreign patients from Israel, the United States, the
United Kingdom, Spain, and Italy and egg sellers from Russia
and Ukraine. The innovation means that no local Cypriots ever
need to know what happens inside the clinic's walls. Most complications to donors only manifest themselves once the women are
back in their home countries.

Despite Verlinsky's admonitions, I drive out to see the Petra
clinic for myself. With its redbrick walls bearing crucifixes and gar-
goyles, it has the look of a partially rehabbed Old World monastery.
I am received by its Russian administrator, Galina Ivanovina. She
was initially reluctant to speak to me, saying that journalists have
purposely and erroneously portrayed the clinic in a bad light. Over
the years several London papers have reported that the clinic intentionally hyperstimulates their donors to produce more eggs than is
safe so that the clinic can split the batches among different patients.
Splitting the batches means that the clinic can reap profits multiple
times for each egg cycle they conduct; however, large batches often
don't produce top-quality eggs and success rates tend to plummet.
A story that appeared in the *Independent* also reported the clinic
offers illegal sex-selection procedures. Another piece in the *Guard-
ian* in 2006 detailed links between Petra and a group of questionably legal fertility clinics in Moscow and Kiev.

The allegations seem to have taken a toll on Ivanovina. She

feels singled out. She starts wringing her hands and speaks in a whisper. She says that if the Petra Clinic has taken liberties with the laws on tissue selling, then it is just as guilty as every other clinic on the island, or for that matter, the world.

She says the women who come to the clinic "do it for economic reasons, nothing else." They get about $500 for their time and potential risk to their bodies; all of the donors come from abroad. Despite the tacit admission of buying eggs, she says that the allegations of overharvesting are false and that at most, batches are only split between two customers. The sellers receive the bulk of their hormone injections before they even arrive, as Petra is only here for harvesting. The staff at Petra is at the mercy of whatever protocols the foreign clinics run. She says she could only recall one patient who reacted negatively to the hormone regimen. It "was a shock, and we sent her immediately to Nicosia for treatment."

I'd heard about the girl's case before. Savvas Koundouros, an embryologist who directs the Genesis Clinic in neighboring Limassol, was on hand when the girl came in. She was on death's door. "What they do is horrible. They get the women sick and then ship them home so that doctors back in the Ukraine can deal with them," he said.

With the clinic in the limelight of suspicion for two straight years, Ivanovina is already preparing for the worst. It almost seems like she expects the police to knock on her door at any minute. She doesn't have to wait long. Three months after my visit the Cypriot police raided the Petra Clinic, accusing the staff of trafficking human eggs. At a press conference in Nicosia the police said that they had taken statements from three women who were flown from Ukraine to be egg donors and that they were illegally paid for their services. But that wasn't the official reason the authorities had it shuttered. They said that the doctors there were licensed only to treat the blood disorder thalassemia, not for egg donation. After the raid Verlinsky conceded that the Petra Clinic "was supposed to be a major center for thalassemia, but centers opened up in other places. There wasn't huge demand. And we saw that people required egg donation." After all, the clinic had its bottom line to consider; it had to provide services where there was demand.

The question at hand, though, was why the police decided to raid the clinic at that moment. In a way, Petra was a perfect target. Owned by foreigners, Petra only performed egg implantation for people who flew in from abroad—scrupulously avoiding local patients as both donors and recipients for human eggs. The exotic nature of the allegations, involving poor Ukrainian women from abroad, showed that the issues were much more thorny than only a licensing irregularity for expanding past thalassemia treatment. At stake wasn't only the question about whether it was right to split the egg donation between international jurisdictions, but what it meant to pay for tissue in general. And busting Petra for illegal harvesting instead of bureaucratic irregularity could put other Cypriot-owned clinics in jeopardy if they have a similar business plan. As Ivanovina pointed out, the problem isn't confined to Petra. Every embryologist in the world has to contend with where to draw the line between compensation and payment. If the human body can't be treated as a commodity, then where are clinics supposed to get raw materials?

.   .   .   .

AS THE WORD *DONOR* SUGGESTS, THE preferred supplier of human eggs is a woman who gives away her eggs in an altruistic act. According to EU law, member states like Cyprus must "endeavor" to ensure voluntary, unpaid donation of human oocytes, though compensation covering lost wages and travel is permissible. The key, says EU health commissioner Androulla Vassiliou, is "where member states draw the line between financial gain and compensation." Customers and suppliers easily get around all this sophistry. "It is twice as difficult to adopt a cat as it is to procure a human egg," writes Glenn McGee, the bioethicist. According to a 2010 study by the European Society of Human Reproduction and Embryology, nearly twenty-five thousand egg donations are performed for European fertility tourists every year. More than 50 percent of those surveyed traveled abroad to circumvent legal regulations at home. There are approximately seventy-six thousand women in Cyprus between the ages of eighteen and thirty who are eligible egg donors. Dr. Trokoudes estimates that each year fifteen hundred of them (or about one in fifty) sell their eggs. The number is staggering. By comparison only one out of every fourteen thousand eligible American women donates.

Perhaps even more alarming is that most of the egg donors in Cyprus come from the relatively small population of poor Eastern European immigrants who are eager to sell their eggs at any price. Though no government statistics break down egg donation in the country, all clinics emphasize their large Eastern European donor pools because their light skin and high education standards make them easier to market to Western European customers. Of the thirty thousand Russians, Ukrainians, Moldavians, and Romanians on the island, some estimates say that as many as one in four have sold their eggs.

Sandwiched between employment ads on the back pages of a weekly Russian-language newspaper is an overture to egg donors. Translated, it reads simply, "An egg donor is needed to help families without children," and a phone number to get in contact with the unnamed clinic. Anyone who reads the ad knows that payment is part of the deal.

While ads like these are common across Cyprus's media landscape, they seem to be less common now than three or four years earlier. It could be that Cyprus is reaching a saturation point where most potential donors have already been recruited and it is a now more difficult to find new sources of eggs. To get over the hump, many clinics now rely on scouts to actively pursue and cultivate potential donors. Natasha, a scout for one of Cyprus's best-known fertility clinics, agreed to meet me to discuss what her job entails on the condition that I changed her name.

Most clinics want Russian donors because Western patients prefer to pass on a lighter complexion to their children, she says. It's a win for the clinics because as immigrants with fewer job prospects, Russians are also easier—and cheaper—to recruit than locals. Natasha, who hails from a small Russian village and came to Cyprus fifteen years ago, describes a typical donor: "She starts a relationship with a Cypriot that she meets on the Internet. And comes here thinking she will have a good life. But in two or three months they have broken up and she has no job, no visa, no place to stay, and no way to get money. For Russians here it is hard to get legal papers, and she needs to make money quickly. All she has is her health and, if she is lucky, she is also quite beautiful." Natasha tells me that in all of her years scouting she has never met a woman who gave up her eggs for any reason other than money.

She says she convinced one woman who got stuck in Cyprus and ended up crashing on Natasha's couch for a month to sell her eggs at a clinic. "She used the money to buy a plane ticket home."

Even doctors sometimes take an active role in filling the donor pipeline. Carmen Pislaru, a Romanian who used to dance in Cypriot and Greek cabarets, says she was still in the hospital recovering from her fourth unplanned child's birth when her doctor, who had helped arrange for the child's adoption, asked if she wanted to sell her eggs. "He knew I was in a desperate position," she says. "I had no money and no way to support my family." Now jobless, she cleans houses for a living, but still carries deep white scars across her cheeks from where a jilted lover attacked her with a knife.

Pislaru says that she turned down the doctor's offer—$2,000 in cash—on the spot. But the relentless physician called her every week for the next month hoping that she'd change her mind. Failing that, he pressured her to put him in touch with women who might say yes. She gave him some names, and several of her acquaintances took him up on the offer. "Many women sell their eggs here to make ends meet. We're all vulnerable," she says.

Peter Singer, the Ira V. Decamp professor of bioethics at Princeton, doesn't necessarily have a problem with selling eggs. "I don't think that trading replaceable body parts is in principle worse than trading human labor, which we do all the time, of course. There are similar problems of exploitation when companies go offshore, but the trade-off is that this helps the poor earn a living," he writes in an e-mail. "That is not to say that there are no problems at all—obviously there can be—and that is why doing it openly in a regulated and supervised manner would be better than a black market."

At the time of writing, the Cypriot Parliament is considering a new law to clamp down on egg trading within the country and institute new, tough penalties to clinics that openly buy and sell human materials. But top embryologists are fighting its passage in fear that it would expose the entire medical community to sanctions.

SAVVAS KOUNDOUROS, THE CYPRIOT surgeon who received the dying egg donor from the Petra clinic, is one of the most popular men on the island, a Cypriot version of George Clooney on *ER*. Men slap him on the back when they meet him; women kiss his cheeks. A handsome embryologist, he has impregnated more women than Genghis Khan. While we stand on a patio on the third story of his high-tech Genesis Centre in downtown Limassol, I ask him how the new law might affect the process of finding egg donors. He lets out a heavy sigh and lights up a cigarette. "What I want to tell you, I cannot tell you," he begins.

All fertility clinics are caught between two opposing ethical dilemmas. "Obviously the donation is described as an altruistic act, which means no payments. But it sounds strange to all of us that a person would receive so many injections over weeks and then undergo general anesthesia just because they are kind people." For him the stakes are huge: In the last year he has invested more than a million euros into constructing a state-of-the-art IVF lab with negative-pressure air locks and three rooms full of impossibly expensive equipment. The investment only makes sense if he can guarantee a supply of eggs for his customers. If Cyprus adopts an altruism-only model and bans all payments to donors, he might not be able to find any eggs to harvest at all.

Consider what happened in the United Kingdom. In 2007 the country went from the cutting edge of the IVF industry to an IVF dead zone when it passed legislation that outlawed even minimal compensation to egg donors. Donor pools that were once plentiful dried up. The wait list for an egg donation in the United Kingdom immediately jumped to two years—an impossibly long wait for women pushing the age limits of safe pregnancy. So British women go abroad when they need eggs. And clinics in Cyprus give women money for their eggs and call it compensation, not payment. They come to the Genesis clinic in droves.

Since the rules are different in every country, most clinics are able to attract customers while hiding in the gray areas of international regulations. Even more important than the laws, though, are the risks associated with egg extraction. Egg donors, though they may not all be informed of it, put their lives on the line with every hormone treatment. Approximately 3 percent of women who undergo IVF develop ovarian hyperstimulation syndrome (HSS), a condition in which the follicles in their ovaries become enlarged and produce too many eggs. If doctors don't throttle down the hormone doses, the condition can prove dangerous. Even fatal—as was almost the case with the Ukrainian woman who nearly died at the Petra Clinic.

Women with polycystic ovaries are particularly susceptible to HSS because their ovaries are swollen into a perpetual state of stimulation. The hormones effectively kick the ovaries into overdrive and deliver many more eggs than normal. Polycystic women are both prized and feared by egg harvesters because while they give more eggs, they also are at increased risk for serious side effects. For some clinics, however, the temptation for extra profits harvested from polycystic donors is too much incentive not to push the limits of safety.

Between 1996 and 1999 that is exactly what an Israeli doctor named Zion Ben-Raphael was accused of doing to his patients without their knowledge. In one case he took 181 eggs from a single unknowing donor, breaking up the batch into lots and selling them to thirty-four paying patients seeking babies. In the course of his tenure thirteen women were hospitalized because of the massive doses of hormones he delivered. Shortly after the scandal was uncovered by the newspaper *Haaertz,* Israel banned all paid egg donation. But the ban sent couples abroad, kick-starting the Petra Clinic's career.

It was just one of a series of similar incidents with Israeli doctors. In July 2009 in Romania, police arrested two Israeli doctors for operating a scheme to bring Israeli fertility tourists to Bucharest for implantation. A sixteen-year-old factory worker was hospitalized and nearly died after selling her eggs to them.

WHILE THE CLINICS OF Cyprus sometime feel like frontier outposts, the ones in Spain seem like established fortresses. Spain has been the top destination for European fertility tourists since the mid-1980s. At Barcelona's Institut Marquès, a fourteenth-century carriage house in one of the poshest areas of town, you can understand why they've made a fortune in the egg business.

Inside, behind sliding-glass doors and whooshing air locks, are two embryology labs where a half dozen workers in blue scrubs and ventilated face masks help turn baby-making from a romantic endeavor into a scientific one. One woman looking at her computer monitor zooms in on an area full of squiggling sperm and a giant human egg. She turns a dial on a control panel and slowly manipulates a microscopic hypodermic needle toward a lone squirming sperm. As it's lined up she presses another button and sucks it up into a chamber off the computer screen. Once there a tiny knife lops off its tail.

"If we cut off the tail it helps the genetic material escape once we implant it into the egg," she says. Then, as if to punctuate the sentence, she thrusts the needle's point through the egg's cell wall and squirts the tiny genetic bundle inside. Presto. Life via laboratory.

This embryo, along with its siblings, has two paths. Two or three of the strongest and most obviously viable will be implanted into a woman who hired the clinic's services, while the five or six excess embryos will sit cooling in a liquid nitrogen bath just in case the first batch doesn't take. Only then will they get a chance to form into something more significant than a bunch of cells.

If one does take and becomes a child then it will probably grow up in Britain. In 2009 the Institut Marquès opened a satellite office in London, offering full-service, pregnancy-guaranteed packages for as little as $37,000 for three IVF cycles. Since each cycle has an approximate 30 percent chance of becoming a viable pregnancy, the overall odds are good.

The stream of foreign customers is so steady that the clinic no longer waits for patients to sign on before tracking down appropriate donors. Instead it keeps a bullpen of women on hormones, ready to give eggs. The clinic simply matches up incoming customers with eggs that are already coming in along the supply chain.

"Sometimes we will lose the eggs if we can't find a customer, but it's a trade-off. This way we can guarantee a steady supply," says Joseph Oliveras, an embryologist at the clinic. The system allows for very short waiting times. It also helps that according to Spanish law, the patient has no control over selecting their donor's characteristics. Matching donors is entirely left to the doctor's discretion, usually by phenotype, but the choice is also probably influenced by availability.

Clinics recruit heavily at Spanish universities and occasionally pepper campuses with flyers. A college diploma is a selling point to customers especially when they can't know much more than this about the donor. However, much more reliable and less talked-about sources of human eggs—especially in Spain, where unemployment soars close to 20 percent—are illegal South American immigrants who have few other options to earn money.

That's fine with most buyers, says Olivia Montuschi, cofounder of Britain's Donor Conception Network, which works with families who have conceived via donated genetic material. (Montuschi's son and daughter were conceived with donor sperm after her husband was found to be infertile.) "The vast majority of women don't care where the eggs actually came from. They are so down the line with unsuccessful fertility treatment at that point that they will go anywhere and do anything."

Nicole Rodriguez (a pseudonym), a Chilean immigrant, says that she sold her eggs to another clinic shortly after arriving in Spain. "We weren't wetbacks—we were students of the visual arts—but I didn't have permission to work yet," she says. "It seemed like easy money." She knew what the clinics wanted. "My skin is a little bit dark, but it was fortunate that it was winter and I was really pale at the time. When I arrived at the clinic, they asked me what my skin color was. I had also put on a lot of makeup, so that they said that my skin was white."

She laughs while recounting her first conversation with a clinic recruiter: "I had asked, 'How much do you pay for eggs?' The woman corrected me, saying, 'You mean your donation of eggs.' I said, 'Yes, excuse me, excuse me—the donation of eggs.'" During the harvesting she chose to undergo general anesthesia. When she woke up, an envelope of cash was lying next to her. "It was like they had thrown cash on a bed stand after seeing a prostitute," she says. The payment of $1,400 was enough for her to live on for four months.

Claudia Sisti, a former patient assistant and international coordinator at the clinic Dexeus in Barcelona, says that these women's experiences are all fairly similar. "Most of the donors were from Latin America; it was easy money for them," she says. Some of the donors even tried to go pro: "One Brazilian woman I knew sold her eggs four or five times in the course of a year and got sick. She was very thin, but they always accepted her into the programs."

Most egg donors I was able to track down independent of the clinics' PR department told similar stories.

A second woman, Kika, an immigrant from Argentina, says that when she gave her eggs she was surprised to see a room full of other South Americans there for the same reason. "They weren't Spanish. They were immigrants. It made me think that this was an immigrant thing, like they were all looking for a way to survive." The injections didn't go well though. "All of the eggs they harvested were too big; the doctors called them super eggs and decided to stop the treatment. They only paid me half the money they promised because they weren't able to get the full batch." The reduced payment gives credence to the argument that the clinic wasn't compensating her for the time and trouble, but the number of eggs they were able to use.

In the end, and despite how clinics and administrators like to talk about it, eggs trade like commodities and move like widgets through supply chains. As the clinics continue to formalize donor recruitment strategies and streamline the pregnancy process, they create a new paradigm for how the world approaches flesh sales. In a way, the human egg is the test case—better than even the kidney—to determine how hospitals will treat commercialization of human tissues if the world tears down barriers on the market.

"The technology is at a point now," says David Sher, founder and CEO of the Switzerland-based fertility service company Elite IVF, "where if you provide sperm, we can basically FedEx you a baby." Most parents, of course, would not see the transaction in such cold and efficient terms. To them, the upside of this poorly regulated marketplace is still miraculous.

Lavi Aron and Omer Shatzky are two gay men living in Tel Aviv. In order to have their marriage recognized in Israel they wed in Toronto in February 2008. But the dream of having children seemed out of reach. "As a gay couple, it is nearly impossible to adopt here," says Aron. "The only real option was to hire a surrogate, but oh, the cost." Friends in similar situations had found the price of surrogacy and egg donation could easily exceed $300,000, and take years of legal wrangling.

But Elite IVF made it comparatively easy as long as the couple was willing to take the procedure global. In the same way that Orbitz searches multiple airlines for the best deals and cobbles together a trip for a lower price, Sher found a Caucasian egg donor living in Mexico City who was willing to give up her eggs.

But Mexico does not have extensive laws to protect the rights of intended parents. So Sher flew a surrogate mother business class from the United States to Mexico for implantation—one sperm came from Aron, the other from Shatzky. The brother and sister were born in California as US citizens in November 2010.

"It was like winning the lottery for us," says Aron. "Genetically, one belongs to him, the other belongs to me. But they're also siblings because they come from the same egg donor. We couldn't have a better family than this; everyone is related to each other." Within weeks Aron and Shatzky were able to arrange legal adoptions for the children and bring them back to Tel Aviv. Total cost: $120,000.

There are many companies that provide similar services to Elite IVF. Together they helped turn baby-making into a globalized, industrialized process where the baby is simply the final product of an informal assembly line. For Sher, who lives in Arizona with his wife, outsourcing is simply the inevitable outcome of the science that allows procreation to move out of the bedroom and into the lab. Like the Petra Clinic and the Institut Marquès, Elite IVF offers clients cheaper access to eggs and a full suite of fertility treatments; unlike those more-localized operations, Elite operates worldwide, with offices and partner clinics in Britain, Canada, Cyprus, Israel, Mexico, Romania, and the United States. Sher plans to expand soon to Turkey, taking advantage of the expected surge of demand there now that the country has banned egg donation.

Sher sees the regulatory and price differentials in eggs as an opportunity to reduce the cost of raw materials and services, and pass the savings on to his customers, offering them virtually any fertility service they can't get at home. Want sex selection, which is illegal in most countries? A Mexican clinic can help you. Too old for IVF in the United States? Cyprus is the answer.

Today Elite IVF's network of clinics, egg sellers, and surrogate moms produces between two hundred and four hundred children per year, helping create families like Aron and Shatzky's. And it's just going to get more complicated. "The future is designer babies," says Sher. He describes an offer that he once received from an investor interested in partnering with Elite IVF. "Surrogates in Asia would carry the eggs of superdonors in America—models with high SAT scores and prestigious degrees who would be paid $100,000 for their eggs. Those babies could sell for $1 million each—first to my investor's friends, then to the rest of the world."

Sher declined the offer, but says that it is only a matter of time until someone moves in that direction. At that point—when the situation is just plain weird—maybe governments will get involved. McGee, the bioethicist, predicts that "we will soon begin to recognize the danger of an ant-trail model of reproduction whereby strangers without responsibility to each other and clinicians able to vanish in a puff of smoke meet in a transaction that culminates in humanity's ultimate act: creation."

For now, we're left to consider Alma Hassina and Yehonnatan Meir, the babies bouncing in the laps of Aron and Shatzky. There is no word to describe their relationship. Born of the same donor, fertilized by the sperm of different fathers, and delivered in the womb of a surrogate mother, they are both twins and half-siblings. They are also poster children for the possibilities enabled by IVF and globalization. Parents will do just about anything for kids like them. Donors will do just about anything for the right price.

The residency unit at the Akanksha Infertility Clinic in Anand, India. These surrogate mothers are kept under close watch during their nine months of pregnancy and usually give birth through cesarean section. Their families are allowed rare visits, and the only obvious source of entertainment in the house is a single television set playing Gujarati soaps. Foreign parents pay about $14,000 to have a child through this clinic. The surrogates earn about $6,000.

CHAPTER SIX
CASH ON DELIVERY

F ROM ITS POCKMARKED exterior walls and stark interior, you'd never guess that this pink three-story building a few blocks from the train station houses India's most successful surrogate childbirth business. But when Oprah raved about the Akanksha Infertility Clinic in the fast-growing city of Anand, it become an overnight success. The clinic fertilizes eggs from donors, implants and incubates embryos in the womb of a surrogate mother, and finally delivers contract babies at a rate of nearly one a week.

Since 2006 Dr. Nayna Patel, Akanksha's founder, has been the subject of dozens of gushing articles in addition to that game-changing 2007 *Oprah* segment, which all but heralded Patel as a savior of childless middle-class couples and helped open the floodgates for the outsourcing of American pregnancies. Autographed photos of Ms. Winfrey are displayed prominently throughout the clinic, which claims to have a waiting list hundreds deep. According to news reports, Akanksha receives at least a dozen new inquiries from potential surrogacy customers every week.

The doctor, clad in a bright red-and-orange sari, sits at a large desk that takes up about a third of the room. Heavy diamond jewelry dangles from her neck, ears, and wrists. Her wide grin projects a mixture of politeness and caution as she beckons me to sit in a rolling desk chair. I showed up here without an appointment, fearing Patel would refuse to see me if I phoned in advance: Despite all the laudatory press, in the weeks prior to my visit a spate of critical articles had appeared, focusing on the clinic's controversial practice of cloistering its hired surrogate mothers in guarded residency units.

Among the claims is that Akanksha is little more than a baby factory. "The world will point a finger at me," Patel responds when I ask her about the criticism. "She will point, he will point. I don't have to keep answering people for that."

As if to prove it, she politely evades my questions for the next twenty minutes, and then abruptly escorts me out when I ask about the residency units again. But in a town as small as Anand, I can track down where the women are without the doctor's assistance.

On a quiet street about a mile away from the clinic, a government ration shop issues subsidized rice to an endless stream of impoverished clients. Across the road is a squat concrete bungalow enclosed by concrete walls, barbed wire, and an iron gate. Police once used it as a storehouse for bootleg liquor captured in Eliot Ness–style raids. (Like the rest of India's Gujarat state, Anand is a dry city.) The security measures were intended to keep away bootleggers who might be tempted to reclaim the evidence.

Now the building functions as one of two residential units

for Akanksha's surrogates. They aren't prisoners here. But they can't just up and leave, either. The women—all married and with at least one previous child—have swapped freedom and physical comfort to enroll as laborers in India's burgeoning medical and fertility tourism industry. They will spend their entire pregnancies under lock and key. A watchman wearing an official-looking uniform and armed with a bamboo cane monitors everyone's movements from the front gate. Visits by family members are limited but, in most cases, they are too poor to make the trip.

Outdoor exercise, even a walk around the block, is a no-go. To get past the guard, the women must have an appointment at the clinic or special permission from their overseers. In exchange, they stand to receive a sum that's quite substantial by their meager standard of living, but that the clinic's foreign customers understand is a steal. Most of the customers come from outside of India, and three of the city's boardinghouses are constantly booked with American, British, French, Japanese, and Israeli surrogacy tourists. Accompanied by my interpreter, I cross the street to the bungalow, where a friendly smile and a purposeful, confident walk get me past the gatekeeper. In the hostel's main living quarters, some twenty nightgown-clad women in various stages of pregnancy lie about, conversing in a hurried mix of Gujarati, Hindi, and a bit of English. A lazy ceiling fan stirs the stagnant air, and a TV in the corner—the only visible source of entertainment—broadcasts Gujarati soaps. A maze of iron cots dominates the classroom-sized space and spills out into the hallway and through additional rooms upstairs. It is remarkably uncluttered given the number of people living here. Each surrogate has only a few personal belongings, perhaps just enough to fill a child's knapsack. In a well-stocked kitchen down the hall, an attendant who doubles as the house nurse prepares a midday meal of curried vegetables and flatbread.

The women are pleasantly surprised to have a visitor. It's rare, one tells me, for a white person to show up here. The clinic discourages personal relationships between clients and surrogates, which, according to several sources, makes things easier when it comes time to hand over the baby.

Through an interpreter, I tell the women that I'm here to learn more about how they live. Diksha, a bright, enthusiastic woman in her first trimester, elects herself spokeswoman, explaining that she used to be a nurse at the clinic. She left her home in neighboring Nepal to find work in Anand, leaving behind her two school-age children. She reasons that she could earn just as much as a surrogate as she could working full-time tending to them. She'll use the money she makes to fund her children's education. "We miss our families, but we also realize that by being here we give a family to a woman who wants one," Diksha says. She and her dormmates are paid $50 a month, she says, plus $500 at the end of each trimester, and the balance upon delivery.

All told, a successful Akanksha surrogate makes between $5,000 and $6,000—a bit more if she bears twins or triplets. (Two other Indian surrogacy clinics catering to foreign couples told me they paid between $6,000 and $7,000.) If a woman miscarries, she keeps what she's been paid up to that point. But should she choose to abort—an option the contract allows—she must reimburse the clinic and the client for all expenses. No clinic I spoke with could recall a surrogate going that route.

Diksha is the only Akanksha surrogate I meet who has an

education to speak of. Most of the women hail from rural areas; for some, the English tutor Patel sends to the dormitories several times a week is their first exposure to anything resembling schooling. But they're not here to learn English. Most heard about the clinic via local newspaper ads promising straight cash for pregnancy.

Among the justifications for cloistering the surrogates—Akanksha isn't the only clinic doing it—is the facilitating of medical monitoring and the providing of better conditions for the women than they might have back home. Kristen Jordan, a twenty-six-year-old California housewife, opted for a Delhi clinic that recruits educated surrogates and doesn't cloister them after she learned that some clinics hire "basically very, very poor [people who are] strictly doing it for the money." For their part, the Akanksha surrogates tell me that their swollen bellies would almost certainly make them the subject of gossip back home. Even so, those who have been on the ward longer than Diksha don't seem terribly thrilled with the whole setup.

I sit down next to Bhavna. She's far along and bulging in her pink nightgown and wearing a gold locket around her neck. She looks older than the rest and more tired. It's her second surrogacy here in as many years, she tells me. Apart from occasional medical checkups, she hasn't left this building in nearly three months, nor has she had any visitors. But $5,000 is more than she would make in ten years of ordinary labor.

I ask for her view of the overall experience. "If we have a miscarriage we don't get paid the full amount; I don't like that," she says. But she's thankful to be here and not at the clinic's other hostel, a few towns away in Nadiad, which isn't as nice. When I ask what happens after she hands over the baby, she replies that the cesarean section will take its toll. "I will stay here another month recovering before I am well enough to go home," Bhavna says. No surrogate I interviewed expected a vaginal birth. Even though C-sections are considered riskier for the baby under normal circumstances and double to quadruple the woman's risk of death during childbirth, the doctors rely on them heavily. They are, after all, far faster than vaginal labor and can be scheduled.

We're joined by a second woman, who has dark brown eyes and wears a muumuu embroidered with pink flowers. I ask them whether they think they'll have trouble handing over their newborns. "Maybe it will be easier to give up the baby," says the second woman, "when I see it and it doesn't look like me."

The clinic isn't that worried about the women keeping the children for themselves and tying up the handoff with legal challenges, but another reason that Akanksha may keep such a close eye on their surrogates is the worry that some of the women may go into business for themselves. In 2008 Rubina Mandal, an ex-surrogate, decided that the Anand model was a perfect platform for fraud. She began posing as one of the clinic's representatives and duping Americans into sending her advance fees for medical checkups.

According to a warning posted on the Akanksha website "Ms. Mandal is not a doctor, she is a fraud and has been known to dupe innocent couples, hence please be mindful in any dealings with her. Moreover, Ms. Mandal may be using our clinic's name in her efforts to lure innocent couples." Below the warning is a grainy black-and-white photo of Mandal wearing a black necklace and impeccably parted hair. The fraud is understandable, if egregious. With so much potential profit in surrogacy, some women want a bigger cut of the action. To date, Mandal has not been apprehended.

INDIA LEGALIZED SURROGACY IN 2002 as part of a larger effort to promote medical tourism. Since 1991, when the country's new procapitalist policies took effect, private money has flowed in and fueled construction of world-class hospitals that cater to foreigners. Surrogacy tourism has grown steadily here as word has gotten out that babies can be incubated at a low price and without government red tape. Patel's clinic charges between $15,000 and $20,000 for the entire process, from in vitro fertilization to delivery, whereas in the handful of American states that allow paid surrogacy, bringing a child to term can cost between $50,000 and $100,000, and is rarely covered by insurance. "One of the nicest things about [India] is that the women don't drink or smoke," adds Jordan, the Delhi surrogacy customer. And while most American surrogacy contracts also forbid such activities, Jordan says, "I take people in India more for their word than probably I would in the United States."

Dependable numbers are hard to come by, but at minimum, Indian surrogacy services now attract hundreds of Western clients each year. Since 2004 Akanksha alone has ushered at least 232 babies into the world through surrogates. By 2008 it had forty-five surrogates on the payroll, and Patel reports that at least three women approach her clinic every day hoping to become one. There are at least another 350 fertility clinics around India, although it's difficult to say how many offer surrogacy services, since the government doesn't track the industry. Mumbai's Hiranandani Hospital, which boasts a sizable surrogacy program of its own, trains outside fertility doctors on how to identify and recruit promising candidates. A page on its website advertises franchising opportunities to entrepreneurial fertility specialists around India who might want to set up surrogacy operations with an endorsement from Mumbai. India's Council on Medical Research (which plays an FDA-like role—except that it has far less power to actually enforce its edicts) predicts that medical tourism, including surrogacy, could generate $2.3 billion in annual revenue by 2012. "Surrogacy is the new adoption," says Dehli fertility doctor Anoop Gupta.

Despite the growth projections, surrogacy is not officially regulated in India. There are no binding legal standards for treatment of surrogates, nor does state or national authority have the power to police the industry. While clinics like Akanksha have a financial incentive to ensure the health of the fetus, there's nothing to prevent them from cutting costs by scrimping on surrogate pay and follow-up care, or to ensure they behave responsibly when something goes wrong.

In May 2009, for instance, a young surrogate named Easwari died after giving birth at the Iswarya Fertility Centre in the city of Coimbatore. A year earlier, her husband, Murugan, had seen a newspaper ad calling for surrogates and pressured her to sign up to earn the family extra money. As a second wife in a polygamous marriage, Easwari was hard-pressed to refuse. The pregnancy went smoothly and she gave birth to a healthy child. But Easwari began bleeding heavily afterward, and the clinic was unprepared for complications. Unable to stop Easwari's hemorrhaging, clinic officials told Murugan to book his own ambulance to a nearby hospital. Easwari died en route.

The child was delivered to the customer according to contract, and the fertility clinic denied any wrongdoing. But in a police complaint the husband suggested that the clinic had essentially dumped responsibility for his dying wife. The official investigation was perfunctory. When I contacted the clinic through e-mail, it took almost half a year to get a response. A doctor from the center wrote that Easwari "developed a severe disseminated intravascular clotting defect," because the child's head was too large. The doctor, who identified himself as Arun Muthuvel, added that the team was unable to save her life despite tearing through seven bottles of blood and calling in additional surgeons. Whether Easwari could have been saved remains a question that only a thorough investigation might hope to answer. However, nobody has the authority to examine such cases, which means that in instances of malpractice patients generally have to take the hospital's word that everything happened according to the highest medical standards. India's Parliament, however, is in the process of crafting legislation to address some of the concerns about surrogacy. The bill could be ready for formal consideration sometime around the end of 2011, but it is not clear which agency would be charged with enforcement.

Any regulatory oversight would likely fall to the states, yet pinning someone down in the government to comment on what department might be able to examine or regulate fertility clinics now is like playing a seemingly endless game of hot potato. It took six visits to different offices in Gujarat's bureaucratic center and phoning three different ministers to get even half an answer: "At the state level, no one looks at surrogacy," says Sunil Avasia,

Gujarat's deputy director of medical services, in a short interview.

When it comes to ethical conduct, it might as well be the Wild West. Forget laws, he says. "There are no rules." That's all he has to offer on the subject. "Perhaps you should talk to my boss," Avasia says. Alas, the boss never returned my calls. Nor has there been an effort to regulate surrogacy contracts on the receiving end. So long as a surrogate infant has an exit permit from the Indian government, the process for getting the baby an American passport is straightforward.

FOR THEIR PART, PATEL'S customers view the residency program as an insurance policy of sorts. "When I was told by my doctor they could get someone in Stockton, [California,] I don't know what they're eating, what they're doing. Their physical environment would have been a concern for me," says Ester Cohen, a forty-year-old from Berkeley who runs a catering company with her husband and teaches Jewish ethics lessons to children on weekends. "The way they have things set up here is that the surrogate's sole purpose is to carry a healthy baby for someone."

I met Cohen in the hallways of the Laksh Hotel, which caters to Akanksha's surrogacy tourists. For many, this Indian excursion represents the final stage of an expensive and emotionally fraught quest for parenthood—their last, best option after a series of failed fertility treatments. Cohen tried for years to conceive, and after extensive testing was told she never would. Adoption didn't appeal to her. Then she read a news article about Patel and knew immediately that she wanted to come to Anand. "Money was definitely one of the reasons, but it was like my gut feeling," she says. "This is where I needed to be." Cohen and her husband decided to keep their undertaking secret from friends and neighbors—at least until they returned home with a baby.

In the United States, a surrogate and her client must establish a relationship before coming to a fertility clinic, but Cohen has barely met Saroj, the woman Akanksha hired to carry her child. They connected just once at the clinic a few minutes after embryos from donor eggs fertilized with her husband's sperm were implanted in Saroj's uterus. That was nine months ago. Cohen has been back in Anand three days now but hasn't gone to visit Saroj. "The clinic wants to keep a separation," Cohen says. "They want it to be clear that this is what her job is: She's the vessel."

But this is where the ethos of commercial surrogacy becomes confusing. Cohen is quick to add that Saroj is giving her one of the most precious gifts one human can offer another. "The clinic won't let someone be a surrogate more than twice, because they don't want them to be just a vessel," she says. "That shouldn't be a job."

Then how to view it? Oprah showcased Jennifer and Kendall, a childless couple who had tried everything else but couldn't afford the American surrogacy system. With Patel's help, Jennifer became a mom, and an Indian woman was lifted from poverty—a transaction that was part business and part sisterhood. The clinics also frame surrogacy this way, insisting that the women offer their wombs out of a sense of communal responsibility, not simply because they need a paycheck.

. . . .

OVER $8 COFFEES AT a swank hotel, Amit Karkhanis, one of Mumbai's most prominent surrogacy lawyers, explains that this language of altruism gives clinics the upper hand in pay negotiations. Meanwhile, the contracts signed by clinic, client, and surrogate are vague about what type of service is being provided. "Is it work? Is it charity?" Karkhanis asks rhetorically, cocking one eyebrow before offering his own opinion: "Surrogacy is a type of employment, plain and simple. Foreigners are not coming here for their love of India. They are coming here to save money." And if surrogacy is being treated as a job, then why aren't women getting market rates for their time in the hospital?

While both cost of living and earning potential are far lower in India than in America, it is still possible to compare the relative pay for surrogates and clinics on either side of the globe: An American surrogate typically gets half to three-quarters of the total paid by the couple, while Akanksha's surrogates receive one-quarter to one-third of the total. Lawyer Usha Smerdon, who runs Ethica, a US-based adoption reform group, told me in an e-mail: "Surrogacy is a form of labor. But it's an exploitative one, similar to child labor and sweatshops driven by Western consumerism. . . . I challenge the notion that within these vastly different power dynamics surrogates are truly volunteering their services, that hospitals are operating aboveboard when driven by a profit motive."

Besides India, only a handful of countries—the United States, Belgium, Canada, Israel, and Georgia—allow surrogacy for pay, and most of those have imposed strict regulations. France, Greece, and the Netherlands forbid even unpaid arrangements, and no country, not even India, recognizes surrogacy as a legitimate form of employment. America leaves regulation to the individual states: Eight recognize and support it, and have mandated health safeguards and counseling for surrogates. Six have banned it outright. And the rest have either deemed surrogacy contracts unenforceable, left surrogacy for the courts to deal with through case law, or simply ignored the practice. India's Council on Medical Research has come up with proposed surrogacy guidelines that caution against some practices already in common use in Anand and elsewhere, such as allowing the clinics to broker surrogacy transactions. But these nonbinding rules, considered a starting point for national legislation, ignore other glaring ethical issues, such as whether it's okay to impose C-sections on a surrogate. Or whether keeping surrogates cloistered under strict medical supervision violates a fundamental principle of personal liberty.

Implantation is another dicey issue. For healthy young women, the American Society for Reproductive Medicine advises American doctors to implant just one—and certainly no more than two—embryos in a woman's uterus per attempt. The Indian guidelines recommend no more than three for surrogates. But Patel's clinic routinely uses as many as five embryos at a time. Using more embryos boosts the success rate but also results in multiple births, which are far riskier for the woman and often lead to premature delivery (by C-section) and dire health problems in the infants. Although it's impossible to verify, Akanksha claims an implantation success rate of 44 percent (similar to other Indian clinics), compared to a US norm of 31 percent. Several of the surrogates I met in Anand were pregnant with twins. In cases where three or more embryos take, the Akanksha clinic selectively

aborts specific embryos to bring the total down to more manageable levels. They do this often without asking permission of the
intended parents or the surrogates.

India's surrogacy guidelines are also silent on the issue of
locking down the women, a practice lawyer Karkhanis believes
is illegal. "The Anand model is completely flawed," he tells me.
"Holding surrogates like that is unlawful confinement under the
Indian Penal Code."

While the guidelines clearly state that "the responsibility of
finding a surrogate mother, through advertisement or otherwise,
should rest with the couple," Akanksha advertises far and wide
for surrogates in local-language newspapers, and many hospitals
have responded to demand by hiring headhunters.

AT MUMBAI'S IMPOSING HIRANANDANI Hospital, physician Kedar
Ganla introduces me to a gaunt woman named Chaya Pagari who
is his direct line to the slums. The forty-year-old "medical social
worker," as Ganla calls her, sits uncomfortably in his office and
meets my questions with hesitation. Given her sparse résumé,
"recruiter" would be a more apt title. Ganla pays Pagari ₹75,000
(about $1,750) for each surrogate he accepts. He's already accepted
three this year, she tells me—meaning she's making more than
the women she recruits. "Between us brokers," she adds, "there is
near constant competition to find surrogates."

Dr. Anoop Gupta does things a bit differently. He runs Delhi-
IVF, the clinic where I met California customer Kristen Jordan,
and where his waiting room is packed with chatty patients. Next
to Akanksha's Spartan vibe, it is night and day, with wood-paneled

walls and a brightly lit aquarium exuding a sense of security and warmth usually lacking in Indian medical facilities.

Clad in green scrubs and a blue hairnet, Gupta is always on the move and has little time for questions. Instead, he has me observe a constant stream of patients who have come to him from as far away as Ireland and California, or from as close as a few blocks away. While most are here for routine fertility treatments, Gupta has at least seven surrogates on the rolls this month. "In India the government makes it difficult to arrange an adoption, while having your own genetic child through a surrogate is legal and easy," the doctor says as he slathers a clear gel on the paddles of an ultrasound machine.* The only hurdle, as he sees it, is finding a surrogate who isn't motivated by desperation. For this, he relies on Seema Jindal, his medical coordinator, who is a licensed social worker and registered nurse at the clinic. Her recruiting method has a twinge of evangelism: "I ask just about every woman I meet socially if she has thought about surrogacy." She focuses on women who have completed college and are well-off enough not to have to rely on the clinic's payments for basic needs. Otherwise, she says, "how do they know they are not being exploited?"

Several months before our interview, Jindal confides, she took a train to Gujarat to snoop on Patel's operation firsthand, both to glean trade secrets that might make her own clinic more profit-

---

* Plagued by scandals like the one I examine in an earlier chapter, adoptions in India have come under increasing regulation that requires more documentation and paperwork. However, there is debate over whether the new rules have done anything at all to decrease instances of trafficking in adoption networks.

able and to scrutinize its flaws. In her view, the residency program treats women like livestock. For the entire length of their pregnancy they only do three things. "They sit, they talk, and they sleep," she says. "It's just not right."

One of Jindal's recruits, a thirty-two-year-old social worker named Sanju Rana, is here for her ultrasound. Unlike Patel's surrogates, she is college-educated and plans to work full-time throughout her pregnancy. She's been promised $7,500 for her services, and has Gupta's direct phone number. During the procedure, Rana, already a mother of two, is surprised to learn that she is carrying twins. She's worried, she tells me, but will most likely carry them to term. "They are good people and have been childless for so long," she says of the American couple who hired her.

Like every other market in human tissue, surrogacy blends notions of altruism and humanistic donation with the bottom line of medical profitability. Expanding the market for surrogate mothers to India certainly allows more Western women to have access to a medical procedure that they would have otherwise been priced out of. However, the new market is simply passing the bill down the line. Before India, only the American upper classes could afford a surrogate. Now it's almost within reach of the middle class. While surrogacy has always raised ethical questions, the increasing scale of the industry makes the issue far more urgent. With hundreds of new clinics poised to open, the economics of surrogate pregnancies are moving faster than our understanding of its implications.

The red market for new children spans the distance between questionable practices in adoption, egg donation, and surrogacy. All three businesses are tied together by our most basic desires for reproduction and raising a happy family. As customers, the intended parents are often unaware of the complexities of the supply chain and can easily enter into dangerous territory unintentionally. All three markets for children are expanding at unprecedented rates, making it easier than ever to buy a child on the red market.

ESTER COHEN IS CHILDLESS no longer. From the day we met in Anand, it took five weeks to finalize her newborn's status as a US citizen, complete with a shiny blue-and-silver passport and a no-objection certificate issued by the Indian government. Cohen has since traded the smog and chaos of Anand for her quiet neighborhood in North Berkeley, where the realities of motherhood have kicked in.

The small apartment she and Adam, her husband, share now feels too cramped, and the couple is looking to move. The electric piano Adam once played daily sits unused in the corner of a room dominated by a crib and assorted baby stuff. As we chat, Cohen bounces Danielle, a healthy blue-eyed girl, on one knee. "It already seems like a thousand years ago that we were in India," she says. "But we are so grateful for what Saroj has given us."

Although Saroj had hoped for a vaginal birth, the clinic delivered Danielle via C-section. "There was an intensity in her eyes," Cohen recalls of the handover. "It was hard for her, and you could see how much she cared for Danielle." In the end, though, the baby had to come home with her mother.

In the basement of Sitla Hospital in Gorakhpur, lab attendants show off a full bag of blood that they recently received from one of the city's five blood banks. A month before this photo was taken, a farmer from a nearby village complained to the police that hospital workers from here kidnapped him and stole his blood by force.

CHAPTER SEVEN
BLOOD MONEY

A FEW DAYS before the Indian celebration of Holi, an emaciated man with graying skin, drooping eyes, and rows of purple needle marks on both arms stumbled up to a group of farmers in the sweltering Indian border town of Gorakhpur. The city is the first stop for many thousands of refugees streaming in from Nepal, a country even more perpetually impoverished than India. Over the years endless refugee hardship stories had dulled the farmers' instincts for sympathy, and junkies were even lower on their list for charity handouts. At first the farmers ignored the man's request for bus fare. But he persisted. He wasn't a refugee, he said. He was escaping from a makeshift prison where his captor siphoned off his blood for profit. The farmers shook off their stupor and called the police.

For the last three years the man had been held captive in a brick-and-tin shed just a few minutes' walk from where the farmers were drinking tea. The marks on his arms weren't the tell-tale signs of heroin addiction; they came from where his captor, a ruthless modern-day vampire and also a local dairy farmer and respected landowner named Papu Yadhav, punctured his skin with a hollow syringe. He had kept the man captive so he could drain his blood and sell it to blood banks. The man had managed to slip out when Yadhav had forgotten to lock the door behind him.

The emaciated man brought the officers to his prison of the last three years: a hastily constructed shack sandwiched between Papu Yadhav's concrete home and a cowshed. A brass padlock hung from the iron door's solid latch. The officers could hear the muffled sounds of humanity through the quarter inch of metal.

They sprung the lock and revealed a medical ward fit for a horror movie. IV drips hung from makeshift poles and patients moaned as if they were recovering from a delirium. Five emaciated men lying on small woven cots could barely lift their heads to acknowledge the visitors. The sticky air inside was far from sterile. The sun beating down on the tin roof above their heads magnified the heat like a tandoor oven. One man stared at the ceiling with glassy eyes as his blood snaked through a tube and slowly drained into a plastic blood bag on the floor. He was too weak to protest.

A crumpled nylon bag next to him held five more pints. Inside were another nineteen empty bags ready for filling. Each had official-looking certification stickers from local blood banks as well as bar codes and a seal from the central regulatory authority.

The room was not unique. Over the next several hours the

cops raided five different squats on the dairy farmer's land. Each scene was as bad as the last, with patients constantly on the verge of death. All told they freed seventeen people. Most were wasting away and had been confined next to hospital-issued blood-draining equipment. In their statements the prisoners said that a lab technician bled them at least two times per week. Some said that they had been captive for two and a half years. The Blood Factory, as it was quickly known in the press, was supplying a sizable percentage of the city's blood supply and may have been the only thing keeping Gorakhpur's hospitals fully stocked.

That evening police rushed the men to the local Civil Hospital to recover. The doctors there said that they had never seen anything like it. Hemoglobin supplies oxygen to various parts of the body, and low levels of it can lead to brain damage, organ failure, and death. A healthy adult has between 14 and 18 grams of hemoglobin for every 100 milliliters of blood. The men averaged only 4 grams. Leeched of their vital fluids to the brink of death, all of them were gray and wrinkled from dehydration. "You could pinch their skin and it would just stay there like molded clay," said B. K. Suman, the on-call doctor who first received the patients from police custody.

Their hemoglobin levels were so low that the doctors were worried about bringing them up too quickly. One told me that they had become physically addicted to blood loss. To survive, the doctors had to give them iron supplements along with a regimen of bloodletting or they could die from too much oxygen in their circulatory systems.

After a few weeks in captivity, the prisoners were too weak from blood loss to even contemplate escape. A few survivors recalled to the police that the original group was much larger, but when Yadhav sensed that a donor was becoming terminally sick, he just put them on a bus out of town so that their deaths would be someone else's responsibility.

Papu Yadhav kept meticulous ledgers documenting the volume of blood that he sold to local blood banks, hospitals, and individual doctors as well as the hefty sums that came back. The notes made it particularly easy for the police to understand the entire operation. Vishwajeet Srivastav, deputy superintendent of police in Gorakhpur in charge of the case, says that the records showed that Yadhav started as a small commercial venture that only propped up his dairy business. In the beginning, at least, he offered a straight deal to the drug-addled and destitute potential donors that he picked up at Gorakhpur's bus and train stations.

The $3 he gave for a pint of blood would buy food for several days. It was illegal, but it was also easy money. Yadhav could easily turn over common blood types for $20 quick profit, while rarer groups could fetch up to $150 a pint. It didn't take long for the situation to deteriorate. As his operation grew, he got tired of trolling the city's transit points. So Yadhav offered the donors a place to stay. With the men under his roof, it was only a matter of time before he took control of their fates though a mixture of coercion, false promises, and padlocked doors.

The blood business got so big that he needed help. He took on a former lab technician named Jayant Sarkar, who had experience running an underground blood farm in Kolkata before he was chased out of the city in the late 1990s. Together Yadhav and Sarkar grew into one of the main blood suppliers in the region.

The business concept was similar to that of Yadhav's milk farm. The two were so interrelated that he kept the cowsheds and human sheds next to each other to economize on space.

Two months after the initial raid the police rounded up nine men: lab technicians who oversaw collection, secretaries at local blood banks who wanted to line their pockets with extra profits, middlemen who ferried blood around the city, and nurses who tended the herd. Smelling trouble, Sarkar was able to escape the city, but Papu Yadhav was captured near his home and served a total of nine months in jail. After a month at Civil Hospital his former captives migrated back to their homes all across India and Nepal.

It is tempting to view the horrors of Gorakhpur's blood farm as an isolated incident: the sort of aberration that only happens on the margins of the civilized world and unrelated to the blood supply anywhere else. But the existence of the blood farm suggests a deeper problem with the circulation of human materials in the market. The blood farm could never have existed without eager buyers who were either incurious about the supply or just didn't care about the source. And once medical personnel were willing to pay money for blood without asking questions, it was almost inevitable that someone would exploit the situation to maximize profit. In fact, the world volunteer blood system is so fragile that a slight hit to the supply could immediately spark the sort of commercial blood piracy that blossomed here.

The entire supply of blood at one blood bank in Gorakhpur, India. These scant stocks are woefully insufficient to treat the constant stream of patients who use the city's hospitals. To bridge the gap in supply, a criminal gang headed by a former dairy farmer began kidnapping men from the bus station and draining their blood by force. Some prisoners stayed locked up for more than three years and had their blood drained more than once a week.

I arrived in Gorakhpur on the eve of Papu Yadhav's release hoping to better understand how a city of two million people became so easily dependent on a blood farm. While the excesses in this city stretch the bounds of the ordinary, the situation was by no means unique to India.

Perched precariously on the border of India and Nepal, Gorakhpur is a mashup of the chaos and pollution of an industrial boomtown and the endemic poverty of rural India. A single rail line and poorly maintained road connect Gorakhpur to the state capital of Lucknow. Still, the city is the central hub for a dense string of villages in what is one of the most densely populated rural areas of the world. Gorakhpur is the only settlement for almost one hundred miles with any sort of urban infrastructure. As such it's an important outpost for the government's presence in the region. The city is in the difficult position of providing basic services for a giant swath of the country, and yet simultaneously being a low development priority. It is a city built on a foundation of shortages.

Worst hit are Gorakhpur's overburdened medical facilities, which are a lifeline to tens of millions of rural farmers and migrant workers. Offering subsidized—and in some cases free—care, the hospitals are magnets for the underprivileged. Even the gigantic Baba Ram Das hospital campus with almost a dozen buildings and a fleet of ambulances has lines of rural patients streaming out the front door. The other major hospitals are even more crowded.

The glut of patients poses several major challenges, especially in the blood supply. Even procedures as routine as birth drive up the demand—a pregnant woman in need of a cesarean section will need at least two pints of blood on hand in case of complications. The millions of migrants who come to the city's hospitals are already sick and in no shape to open up their veins. There are simply too few good candidates for blood donation.

It's a perfect storm for the worst forms of medical malpractice and ethics. There are no opportunities for the comparatively small local population to replenish the stocks of blood through voluntary donations, so hospitals have little choice but to rely on the underground machinations of local blood dealers.

A blue-and-white neon sign hanging a five-minute walk from Papu Yadhav's former blood farm announces Fatima Hospital, one of Gorakhpur's five blood banks. There, a patchwork of concrete rubble and construction debris lies just inside the hospital's iron-and-brick gateway, as the hospital is in shambles while undergoing a major renovation. But the blood bank was too important to put off or leave nonfunctional during the renovation. So the Jesuit church that is financing the construction saw to it that the blood bank was finished first. But for now, that means avoiding stray cats, picking my way across piles of rebar and sand, and climbing unfinished stairways to get to the hematology department.

But once I'm inside it's like being in a different world. The place is packed with state-of-the-art equipment, including a sub-zero refrigerator that can store blood almost indefinitely and shiny new centrifuges that can separate blood into its component parts. The unit is the brainchild of Father Jeejo Antony, who runs the hospital for the local diocese. However, all the high-tech gear in the world won't help his main problem. He tells me that they barely collect enough blood to meet his own hospital's needs, let alone the city's. The problem, he says, is that most people in India won't give blood voluntarily. He says that many local people here are superstitious and believe that losing bodily fluids will make them weak for the rest of their lives. This is partly why the city began depending on professional donors.

"Papu Yadhav is only a scapegoat. There are many more people behind the blood sales than low-level people like him," he says when I bring up the case, adding, "There are agents in every nursing home and every hospital. When a doctor requests blood, it gets arranged somehow."

After showing me around the lab, he leads me to his expansive office downstairs and offers me a cup of spiced chai. When we're comfortable he tells me that he moved to Gorakhpur from his home state of Kerala to make a difference in people's lives, but he's unsure that anything he does with a voluntary blood bank is going to lessen the pressure. In fact, he says other people have come up to replace the Yadhav gang. One week after the police arrested Yadhav, requests for blood at the blood bank spiked 60 percent. But now, a year later, "the demand has fallen off." There are no new blood banks in the city, and no sudden influx of donors, but blood is coming from somewhere.

Legal blood donation works slightly differently in India than it does elsewhere in the world. Since few Indians are willing to donate through pure altruism, patients are expected to provide their own donors to give blood to a blood bank to replace the pints that they will use during surgery. Once the patient has received credit for a blood donation through a friend, they can draw a matching unit for their own surgery. In theory this means friends and family must step forward to come to the patient's aid. But the reality of the system is different. Instead of asking their relations

to give blood, most people rely on an informal network of professional donors who hang out in front of hospitals willing to give
blood in return for a small fee.

Father Antony says that there is little he can do to stop the
blood selling. Hospitals are caught in a double bind between saving the lives of patients on the operating table and potentially
exploiting donors. From the clinical perspective, when a patient
is dying on the operating table, buying blood seems like the
lesser of two evils. He tells me that his hospital is too small to
attract semiprofessional donors, but all of the major hospitals in
the city have them. A good place to start, he says, would be the
same hospital that treated Papu Yadhav's prisoners after their
rescue by police.

DR. O. P. PARIKH, director of Gorakhpur's Civil Hospital, has
donated thirteen pints of blood in his life and would like to donate
four more before he retires at the end of next year. Yet he says that
he is the exception to the rule. The rest of the city is not as giving as he is. Responsible for the overall operation of the hospital,
he says that blood supply is a constant problem. "People here are
afraid of donating. They don't want to exchange blood; they just
want to buy it." And at ₹1,000, or about $25 for a pint, it isn't hard
to find donors.

Fifty feet outside of Parikh's door is a string of makeshift tea
shops and cigarette sellers who double as blood brokers. After
a discreet inquiry with a man with *paan* stains across his lower
teeth, I'm told to meet a man named Chunu, who is the resident
professional donor. "Just be sure that you trade it in at the bank.
He's got HIV; the blood isn't always screened," the man warns

before sending me on my way. Five minutes later I'm in an alley behind the hospital face-to-face with a small, bearded man holding a shawl over his head and ears. I tell him I need a pint of B negative blood as quickly as possible.

"B negative is rare and difficult to find these days," he says. "You can get it but we need to send for it from Faizabad or Lucknow," two district capitals about one hundred miles from here. He says he could arrange it for ₹3,000, a high figure. I tell Chunu that I will think about it and leave him outside the hospital gate to speak with other customers.

Civil Hospital's blood bank is a picture of helplessness. The steel refrigerator containing blood packets is close to empty, with only three packets ready for transfusion. The blood bank's director, K. M. Singh, says, "Yesterday someone came in and asked for blood, but we had to turn them away. I tell them that blood is not for sale; you have to give it to get it. But they went away and came an hour later with a donor. How am I to know if they paid that person?"

Gorakhpur's five blood banks can only fulfill about half the required demand. Responsible for providing their own blood for operations, patients sometimes don't even know that they are breaking the law when buying blood.

The maternity ward at Baba Raghav Das Hospital, the city's largest government medical institution, is a dismal place to bring life into the world. A coat of translucent green paint on the giant bay windows, put there presumably to reduce the glare, bathes the concrete wards in a sickly light. In the cramped ward about fifty women, still wearing the clothes they brought from home, recover from cesarean sections on thin cots. Some have beds, while others are forced to recline on the concrete floor.

There are dozens of newborns in the room, yet oddly none of them seems to be crying. It is as if the place's cavelike qualities swallow up all the sound. A woman coddling a baby girl adjusts her robe before removing her own catheter and draining a red soupy mixture into a wastebasket below her bed. Despite the conditions, BRD offers these people a rare chance to see a doctor. The wards are just one of the prices they pay for access to medical assistance.

One migrant, Gurya Devi, has traveled more than one hundred miles from a farming village in the neighboring state of Bihar because she feared there might have been complications during labor. A doctor who never told her his name spent a total of five minutes meeting with her. He said that she would need a cesarean section. As a precaution, he said they would need a pint of blood on hand, and could get a donor for ₹1,400 (about $30). "It was easy," she says. "We didn't even have to think about it; the doctor arranged it all."

The blood could have come from anywhere.

RELYING ON PROFESSIONAL DONORS is dangerous for both donors and recipients. British sociologist Richard Titmuss, whose exposition on the blood trade transformed donor systems in the West, was mentioned in the introduction of this book; he predicted that paid blood would not only create a commercial incentive to lower ethical standards in order to increase the supply, but would decrease overall quality of the blood in blood banks. In his book

The Gift Relationship, he studied the spread of hepatitis in blood
banks in the United States and Europe and anticipated the con-
tamination of the international blood supply by viruses like HIV.
While his conclusion, relying only on altruism in blood exchanges,
has possibly fueled a black market for human tissue, he correctly
illustrated how a financial incentive can force people into making
irresponsible health-care decisions.

The blood seller I met outside Civil Hospital was willing to
sell allegedly HIV-infected blood to a passerby as long as he made
a small amount of cash. It's not hard to see how the breakdown in
blood-supply regulation could fuel an epidemic.

Until 1998 blood selling wasn't only legal in India, it was
a mainstream career option with a powerful trade union and
commercial donor rights organizations. When India switched
to an all-voluntary policy, the price of blood shot up from about
$5 a pint to almost $25, a figure that remains out of reach for
many ordinary patients. While the laws changed to make paid
blood illegal, the country was unable to create an alternative
system. The shortage stretches across all the medical industries
that depend on a steady supply of blood. The need for blood
components—both red blood cells and clotting factor, which is
used to treat hemophiliacs—exploded, and India had to start
importing an annual $75 million worth of blood components
from abroad. (Oddly enough, many of those components origi-
nate from US blood donors. The United States is one of the largest exporters of blood in the world, with an export industry that
grosses billions of dollars a year.)

In India the problem isn't that there is a lack of laws meant
to regulate the buying and selling of medical services, but a near

total absence of a plan to collect blood in an ethical manner or at a scale that will meet the nation's needs. The vacuum between legal mandates and police priorities creates an opportunity for a black medical market to flourish.

The free-for-all in Gorakhpur is just an extreme example of a fundamental conflict playing out between private and public medicine the world over. The situation had a parallel in the United States during the transition from the socialized medicine of the New Deal to the for-profit models that have dominated since World War II.

Up until the 1950s in the United States most hospitals were charitable institutions often affiliated with the government. Medical bills were paid out of pocket or were vastly subsidized by the government. The age of for-profit medicine propelled by private insurance policies was only beginning by the time President Eisenhower was in office. But institutions learned that some people would pay a premium for more sophisticated care. Private hospitals staffed with specialist doctors whose advanced knowledge was a scarce commodity started to replace the massive public institutions mostly staffed by general practitioners.

The blood supply went through similar managerial changes. In World War II soldiers on the front line needed massive quantities of blood to help repair their wounds. Highly perishable, whole blood would not keep for a transatlantic voyage. To find an alternative, the Red Cross helped popularize centrifuge technology that could separate red blood cells from blood plasma. Although it doesn't have hemoglobin, plasma adds needed volume to a person's circulatory system during surgery, and is a key factor when treating bleeding wounds. Just as important, plasma has a longer shelf life than whole blood and can better survive a long overseas journey. Plasma allowed Americans to donate massive quantities of blood voluntarily, and citizens felt that they were doing something very specific to save a soldier's life on the front lines. Richard Titmuss was inspired by the United States' and Britain's home war effort to aid their armed forces and wrote that blood donation gives the donor a sense of purpose and solidarity in times of national crisis.*

During the war, surgeons got used to operating with larger available supplies of blood and developed more complex surgical techniques that greatly advanced the field of surgery. After the war the demand for blood remained high as doctors transferred their battlefield knowledge to the civilian sector. But without a war effort to inspire donation, the country needed a more efficient system for blood collecting.

Between the 1940s and 1960s paid blood collection centers coexisted unsteadily with unpaid voluntary donation spots. The class differences were stark. The paid collection points mostly set up shop near skid-row shantytowns while volunteer programs ran blood drives at churches and maintained welcoming centers in more respectable parts of town. There were clear differences in quality as well. Driven by monetary incentives, paid donors were not concerned with the safety of their contributions, only the paycheck that came after donating. The blood collection points also skimped on cleanliness. Titmuss noted

---

* On September 11, 2001, tens of thousands of Americans all signed up to donate blood at once. Hospitals had to turn people away. Now, on the anniversary of the attacks, hospitals run bustling blood drives across the country.

that paid donors had higher frequencies of blood-borne diseases. He wrote that hospitals depending on for-profit blood banks contributed to the spread of hepatitis through transfusions. The instances were significantly lower when people volunteered their blood. Journalists covering blood banks at the time noted that the conditions at the for-profit locations were shabby, sometimes with dirt floors and crumbling walls and "worms all over the floor."* The focus was on harvesting blood, not the condition of the donor.

For-profit blood banks were making money even when they were selling infected blood, but the discrepancy in quality was not lost on doctors. In some cities doctors were so alarmed at the risks of using infected blood that they directed their hospitals to buy only from volunteer blood banks. Sensing danger to their business model, the for-profit centers fought back. Private banks began to systematically sue the hospitals for violating American antitrust laws. They argued that since blood was an openly traded commodity, volunteer blood donation constituted unfair competition for raw materials. The doctors' clinical decisions set patients' health on a collision course with corporate interests.

Most famously, in 1962 in Kansas City, two commercial blood banks took their case before the Federal Trade Commission and won an injunction against nonprofit hospitals' use of volunteer blood. In the decision the hospitals were fined $5,000 for every day that they continued to depend on the safer supply of blood. The majority decision by the FTC stated that the nonprofit Com-

---

* Richard Titmuss, *The Gift Relationship*, 160.

munity Blood Bank, along with hospitals, pathologists, and doctors, were "illegally joined in a conspiracy to restrain commerce in whole human blood."

In the years that followed, the American Medical Association fought repeated battles against the Federal Trade Commission's precedent and was eventually able to overturn the action. But the ruling remained constantly on the minds of many in the medical community who cautioned that the privatization of medicine would create similar problems in other markets for human tissue. They worried that commercial pressures would give incentives to doctors to provide unnecessary treatments.

At the same time as Kansas blood banks were fighting for the right to sell blood from commercial blood donors, the Arkansas Department of Corrections entered into agreements with pharmaceutical companies and hospitals to sell blood plasma taken from inmates. The program helped subsidize the price of incarceration and increased the supply of blood in the state, but at a great cost. The prison system had little incentive to screen the donors for quality, and over the thirty years that the system was in effect, Arkansas blood was linked to outbreaks of hepatitis and contributed to the early spread of HIV. One of the highest-volume buyers of Arkansas blood was a Canadian blood supply company that routinely disguised its sources in order to increase its sales. Without knowing its source, buyers imported diseased plasma around the world, spreading infected blood as far as Japan, Italy, and the United Kingdom.

Eventually the United States and Canada restricted the practice, and finally in 1994, almost a decade after the uniform law against organ trafficking was passed, Arkansas became the last state to outlaw the sale of prisoner blood. Subsequent investigations conservatively estimated that in Canada alone one thousand people contracted HIV through infected blood and another twenty thousand got hepatitis C.

In the context of the rest of the world, Gorakhpur isn't so much an anomaly as a regression to earlier blood scandals. And with shortages in one area, it is easy to see the problem spread out across the entire medical system. Even after Papu Yadhav's crime spree, the drastic shortages were ample incentives for other sorts of criminal schemes to increase the overall supply. Today the problem doesn't just take place behind padlocked doors but also on the streets.

The government-run hospital where Gurya Devi delivered her child has to at least make an appearance of propriety. Its private counterparts are under no such pressure. With only three government hospitals, private clinics are where anyone with a little money goes to receive quicker though not necessarily better service.

The city's medical infrastructure is a mishmash of backroom clinics and private hospitals. Advertisements for cheap pharmaceuticals line every block and seem to grow almost organically like vines up traffic poles and streetlights. By sheer volume, Gorakhpur sells more pharmaceuticals than New Delhi. Since it's so close to the Nepalese border—where hospitals are even worse—smugglers and patients carry massive amounts of drugs back to the neighboring country. While care is similar among the government hospitals, the quality of private clinics varies wildly. The places with good reputations have long lines of turban-clad farmers and their emaciated wives circling around the block. They will wait all day for a visit with a respected clinician. Other clinics strive to attract even a single patient in a day. And in many cases the competition over patients can get violent.

Kedar Nath spent much of his life in the small village of Kutwahan farming a patch of dirt for rice, mangoes, and bananas. His face is worn and wrinkled from sixty years of honest work. Three of his sons have gone on to work migrant construction jobs in faraway Mumbai and send a small amount of money home each month to keep the lights burning. Nath stays frugal so that he can stow away something for when he is too old to tend to his land. When I meet him the weather-beaten farmer is wearing a white dhoti and sun-bleached turban. His hands are knotted with age, but his eyes are lively like a young man's.

He also has a host of health problems that put him on a worn-down public bus to Gorakhpur once a month. His doctor, Chakrapani Pandey, is often found on the American lecture circuit, but has dedicated his life to serving the poor, operating a heavily subsidized clinic in the center of town. He's one of the most respected physicians in Gorakhpur. Every morning the line of patients for his services begins to form three hours before office hours.

In March 2009 Nath hired a three-wheeled auto rickshaw to take him from the bus station to Pandey's office. The driver had different plans. When Nath got in the backseat, two muscled men with betel-stained teeth and fierce faces told him that they would take him to a better doctor. "They said Pandey didn't know what he was doing, and that people at Sitla Hospital were better," he tells me. When he protested, the men grabbed his arms and held him down. When he cried out for help nobody listened.

Sitla Hospital is just one of many new private clinics that cater to migrant laborers. Inside, four stories of waiting rooms and operating theaters offer a range of general services, but like anywhere in Gorakhpur, it has a near-constant shortage of blood.

Nath says he was dragged up the concrete ramp to the hospital and forced to pay a fee at the front counter. The men then dragged him to a small private room with an iron door. "Then there were four men, and they held me down, one man on each limb," he says with anger hotly flashing across his face. "I was helpless." One of the attendants plugged a needle into his arm and drained about a pint of blood into a glass container. When the procedure was over, his white dhoti was stained in blood and they threw him out onto the street with a prescription for a urinary infection. He partially blacked out from exertion and blood loss, and it took him close to an hour to regain his feet. When he could finally stand he hired a rickshaw to take him to Pandey.

A HEFTY MAN WITH a kind face, Pandey sits behind a massive iron desk with a ceiling light that hangs from a thin white wire until it is lower than his eye level. The only hint of luxury is a massive air conditioner that blasts cold air until the office approaches arctic temperatures. At the mention of Kedar Nath's name his face falls and he lowers his voice.

"You have seen the lines outside my office—everyone in the city knows I am a popular doctor. But I lose at least three patients a day to agents of other hospitals who want to add to their business," he says. In Gorakhpur, he says hospitals don't only compete for blood supplies but warm patient bodies as well. They hire taxi drivers and small-time thugs to stake out other clinics and bring patients—sometimes by force—to commission-paying hospitals. Once, he says, he was able to catch one of the agents, who told him that commissions could reach up to ₹3,000 ($75) for an ailing patient who might generate large fees for a hospital. The small fortune is enough to make any taxi ride fraught with danger.

"With Kedar they stole his blood. Who knows what else these people are capable of?" he asks. Or, for that matter, what other crimes are committed in the name of medicine?

The identification card I used during a clinical trial for the experimental erectile dysfunction drug Levitra. In 2005 I was locked in a small testing facility along with broke college students and professional lab rats and dosed to test the maximum safe level for the drug.

CHAPTER EIGHT
CLINICAL LABOR
OF GUINEA PIGS

I AM THE Chuck Yeager of erectile dysfunction. Or, at least, one of them.

In the summer of 2005, fresh out of a graduate program in anthropology at the University of Wisconsin–Madison, my meager student stipend was about to run out. I was uninsured and already in debt from student loans. For me, and thousands of students across America, one of the surest ways to make a quick buck is to sign up to be a human guinea pig for a drug trial. Madison is one of a handful of major clinical testing centers in America, and renting out my body was as easy as perusing the classifieds section of the local weekly paper, right next to the ads for escorts and no-strings-attached personals.

Like prostitution, the cash was enticing. The $3,200 that Covance, a local contract research organization that runs clinical trials on behalf of major pharmaceutical companies, advertised on its website seemed like a great deal. In only a few weeks I could earn as much as I usually made in three months. The drug in question was a reformulation of Viagra, one of the highest-grossing drugs of all time.

At the time, Pfizer had a lock on the erectile dysfunction market, and Bayer Pharmaceuticals wanted a slice of the pie. Bayer's proposed erectile enhancer was a subtle reformulation for what in industry jargon had come to be known as a "me too" drug: one that has the same basic pharmacological properties as something already on the market, but different enough to be eligible for a separate patent. "Me too" drugs still have to clear regulatory hurdles, and Bayer hired the CRO Covance to run the clinical trials. After a brief screening process, Covance, hired me and about thirty other men to spend four weekends together in a room hopped up on massive doses of penis stiffeners.

Of course, I'd be getting paid, but clinical trials aren't exactly safe. In 2006 eight volunteers enrolled in a week-long study of TGN1412, an experimental drug that was being tested to treat rheumatoid arthritis and leukemia. Within minutes of the first dose six men vomited and lost consciousness. The staff at Northwick Park Hospital in London rushed them to the trauma unit, where doctors recognized the symptoms of multiple organ failure. The doctors saved their lives, but the drug had irreversibly damaged their immune systems. One lost his toes and fingers. Another eventually developed a cancer that may have been triggered by the drug.

In 1999 in Philadelphia the stakes were even higher. Jesse Gelsinger died five days after receiving one of the first gene-therapy cocktails when he was only eighteen years old. Gene therapy offered exciting prospects to combat genetic disorders by targeting specific changes in a patient's genetic makeup and swapping out bad genes for good ones. If the drug had worked it might have been a first step in a whole new field of revolutionary medicine. But his death had a chilling effect. The media branded the entire field of gene therapy a dead end, and the outrage effectively closed off a promising direction of scientific inquiry. The FDA and investors were so shaken by his death, it took ten years for another gene therapy clinical trial to move ahead. The fallout from that trial hangs over every other modern experiment and raises the stakes for pharmaceutical development. If a drug study goes bad, not only could someone die, but billions of dollars in investment could suddenly turn worthless.

But a dose of rebranded Viagra didn't seem so dangerous. After all, millions of people were already using it around the country. When I first reported for duty at the squat one-story complex outside the city, I entered through an air lock and a nurse signed me in, told me where to drop my bags, and hung a photo ID around my neck. I made my way through hallways and common rooms that smelled strongly of latex and antiseptic, passing men in their thirties from another study holding small pads of blood-stained gauze in the crooks of their arms. The bandages resembled miniature renditions of Japan's national flag.

An hour after the last stragglers for the Levitra trial arrived, the head nurse marshaled the volunteers into the dining room and listed the house rules:

1. Always ask permission before going to the bathroom, since subtle changes in the bladder could alter Levitra's metabolization rate.

2. Show up for blood draws on time. No exceptions. There
   would be nineteen draws a day.
3. No booze, sex, caffeine, drugs, porn, or exercise. In fact, the
   less we actually did other than process the drug, the better.
4. Report any unusual side effects immediately.

"This is basically a feed and bleed study," the nurse told us.
"We're trying to find out how long the drug stays in your system.
We don't need to know if you have an . . . um . . . we don't need
to know if the drug is having its desired effect—only if it's abnor-
mal." To our relief we interpreted that as meaning she wasn't
interested in our erections. After we filed out of the audience hall,
I sat down on a couch in front of a giant television and shook
hands with the other members of the study, at least half of whom
did this for a living.

One of them, a forty-four-year-old veteran of almost fifty clinical trials named Frank, had traveled here by bus from Florida. He
was wearing blue sweatpants and a faded Champion T-shirt—a
uniform that screams comfort over style. He told me that the trick
to getting through is to remain calm with the superficial discom-
forts. I'd know if things went seriously wrong.

Once, he told me, he saw someone freak out during his first
blood draw. The test subject started screaming that the experimental cocktail was burning his arm and that he wanted out. The
nurse gave him the option of leaving right then and there, "but he
would have had to forfeit his stipend." The patient ran. But Frank
decided to stick with it. There was no way he was going to give up
easy money. They dosed him, and he felt the same burn the guy
before him did. But instead of panicking, he was content.

Within days the doctors called off the study and sent the compound back to the lab for reformulation. "It felt like a hustle. Those of us who stuck it out got paid for the full thirty-day study with only a few days in the clinic," he tells me with a smirk. He didn't know if he had damaged any part of his body, but staying put earned him an easy $8,000.

If it was a hustle, what kind of hustle was it? On a drug trial test subjects don't work in a traditional sense; many even talk about their experiences as if they are a source of free money. However, just because they're not actively working doesn't mean that they're not providing a valuable service to drug companies. The product these human lab animals are offering doesn't come from physical or mental exertion, but it is both potentially dangerous and time-consuming. Puzzling over this issue, social anthropologists Catherine Waldby and Melinda Cooper coined the term *clinical labor* to describe the not-quite-work that Frank does for a living. Without their valuable contributions the entire pharmaceutical business could grind to a halt.

The official stance of the drug industry is that there should be no such thing as clinical labor. Volunteering for a drug study has the same mix of altruism and profitability that exists in every other of the world's red markets. While drug companies begrudgingly compensate people for the time they spend in a clinical trial, they reiterate that guinea-pigging is not a job. It's a donation.

That doesn't stop almost fifteen thousand people in the United States from making a substantial portion of their income through drug trials. The Internal Revenue Service doesn't see a problem with it either and happily taxes the cash that the companies pay out.

Unlike, say, working in a sweatshop, providing accounting services, or engaging in prostitution, a test subject doesn't have to *do* anything. The pharmaceutical companies are simply renting their bodies in order to study metabolic processes. Laboratories pay for the time it takes test subjects to go through trials and to offset the potentially serious risks to test subjects' health.

From the perspective of the quality of the data, relying on professional guinea pigs is a problem. For the best results doctors need to isolate as many variables as possible—something made problematic when test subjects move from trial to trial, accumulating an unknown mix of experimental compounds in their system. People who have been doing it for a long time can become so used to processing drugs that their immune systems might react erratically in ways not found in the normal world. That's why in an ideal setting a test subject has had little or no prior exposure to drugs. In the best trials, test subjects are genuinely *treatment-naive,* that is, they have literally no medical histories to speak of. The blanker the subject's slate, the easier it is for a drug company to transform the data from their bodies into dollars.

As a rule, professional guinea pigs have their own interests ahead of the data's. This sense of self-preservation can skew results. Testers try to game the system by not taking drugs or pushing studies dangerously close together. Too many spurious drug interactions, and a trial might have to restart from the beginning.*

---

* For an excellent analysis of the clinical trial lifestyle as well as the penchant that the drug business has for doctoring data, see Carl Elliott's groundbreaking book *White Coat, Black Hat: Adventures on the Dark Side of Medicine* (Boston: Beacon Press, 2010). His analysis of drug industry charlatans, professional lab rats, and corruptible practitioners will make you very wary of your medicine cabinet.

At the same time, pharmaceutical testers are in a double bind. Clinical testing is dangerous work by its nature, and testing centers have trouble filling their rosters with willing bodies. Real volunteers acting out of pure altruism are rare. But paying cash means that professional testers are almost inevitable. The alternative is to bring back the earlier-era model for recruiting subjects. Between World War II and the 1970s an estimated 90 percent of drugs were first tested in prisons. Inmates had little choice when it came to volunteering—they could either choose hard labor or sign up as lab rats. Prisons allowed the drug companies to closely monitor the prisoners' every movement and could rely on the state to keep them from cheating.

The strict protocols led to a blossoming of drug development with highly accurate data at a fraction of the cost of modern counterparts. But eventually prisoners' rights activists were able to ban the practice. They compared the dangers of inmate drug studies to the Tuskegee syphilis studies of the 1930s through the 1970s, in which a control group of poor black invalids had been intentionally left untreated by doctors while testing the efficacy of antisyphilis medications. When prisons were banned as test sites, drug companies lost their entire base of testable human flesh and had to retool their research strategy to favor incentives rather than coercion.

Paid volunteers replaced prisoners. And soon an entire class of people—mostly blue-collar workers, ex-prisoners, students, and immigrants—found that drug trials could be its route to financial independence. The situation left drug companies in an uncomfortable position.

A veteran test recruiter quoted in an article by the anthropologist Adriana Petryna said that recruiting is a perennial problem:

"I don't know anyone who has really cracked the code. Sometimes you get lucky and fill a study quickly, but for the most part
patients are really difficult to find, and they are difficult to find
because everybody is looking for them."[*]

IN THE COMMON ROOM of the drug trial, Frank told me that he's a
true veteran of the business. Tall, with a mop of unkempt black hair,
he was nearing the end of his clinical trial run. He told me that the
trick to making a career on clinical trials is not completely straight-
forward, but that there is a certain stretch of test centers running
from Miami to Seattle that lab rats migrate between like seasonal
laborers. "Ideally a lab rat shoots for one trial every other month so
that they can get the medication out of the system. That gives you a
thirty-day safety margin for any unexpected interactions," he said.
And besides, the pros (who are mostly composed of ex-convicts, illegal workers, or students) are in it for the quick money.

    And one more thing: "If you keep doing this you are going
to have to take care of your veins, or you will look like a junkie."
And looking like a junkie is a sure way to get kicked out of future
studies. He told me how to rub vitamin E on the punctures to
speed up healing and to switch arms whenever possible. "It hurts
the first time you get stuck with a needle, but between the third
and tenth time you don't care anymore. After a year of studies you
want to take the needle from the phlebotomist and do it your-

---

[*] Adriana Petryna, "Ethical Variability: Drug Development and Globalizing Clinical
    Trials," *American Ethnologist* 32, no. 2 (2005): 185.

self. With trainees it's not even a question. They'll slice you like a razorblade." For full-time testers, their veins earn the paycheck. And without a delivery method to his circulatory system Frank wouldn't make a living.

With all that in mind, I felt ready on the second day of the study at 6:45 in the morning when I got my first dose of the drug. They gave me a small bowl of cornflakes, whole milk, and fifteen minutes to finish up before asking me to line up with a subset of the total group. We understood that the entire study was being staggered between placebos, middling doses, and high doses of Levitra. I made eye contact with Frank and smiled at him. He eyed the nurses' station with practiced ease, like a race car driver analyzing a track.

The stick went easily and the pretty young nurse who drew the morning shift sent me on my way to the head matron, who was wearing a dour look. The matron was seated at a desk. Standing on her right was someone holding a flashlight. In front of them was a blue paper towel with a single pill on it and a glass of water.

"Put the pill on your tongue and drink the whole glass of water. Be sure the pill goes down. Hiding it in your mouth will disqualify you from the study." I realized that Frank probably had similar tricks up his sleeve for getting through trials unfazed. I downed the pill and the woman searched my mouth with the light and had me move my tongue just to be sure.

The current formulation of Levitra is administered in 2, 5, 10, and, for the most severe cases, 20 mg doses. I got 30 mg. The high dose was meant to test the upper limits of human endurance to be sure that the millions who take the drug down the line aren't poisoning themselves. For lab rats, however, testing the limits of poisoning is the name of the game. Perhaps 30 mg is enough to make someone's penis fall off. Nobody wants that.

I eventually meet up with Frank and I ask him if he took the pill. He tells me that pros can definitely hide drugs, but it's not worth it for what we're taking.

"The 'me too' drugs are the safest. Nothing to worry about." I almost trust Frank that there is little danger. It was just a subtle twist on Viagra. And both drugs are really just a blood-flow redirector. What harm could it do?

To get approval a drug needs to pass through three phases of clinical research trials. The most dangerous is Phase I, where a small group of volunteers take high doses of an experimental drug to test its toxicity on healthy patients. This phase represents the highest allowable dose that a doctor should prescribe. Phase II happens on a larger group of sick patients and tests its effectiveness in treating a specific condition; and finally the massive Phase III trials are the safest and ultimately decide the drug's clinical application. Professional test subjects rarely venture out for anything other than the most dangerous and high-paying trials.

THE TRIAL IN MADISON was Phase I, and it didn't take me long to realize that I was testing the upper limits of human endurance of erectile interactors. Within an hour my head started throbbing like it had been split down the middle. I fell into bed and kept the lights low. Finding the maximum permissible level means that the clinicians have to constantly skirt the line of safety, ratcheting down the dose only after inching it into the danger zone. In the hallways, beneath unforgiving fluorescent light, I could hear one of the other lab rats puking. He vomited into a toilet for a half hour, while nurses behind a Plexiglas barrier monitored his progress.

He asked for an Advil, but the nurse replied through an intercom that she needed to get permission from her boss before she could give him any treatment. She didn't want to skew the data. Permission for the headache reliever made its way down the chain of command only after three hours.

Of the men in the study only two didn't get headaches, putting the upper threshold of practically using this erectile dysfunction drug below 30 mg. The waiting room was full of both headaches and erections—not a particularly sexy combo.

I was still scheduled to come back for two more weekends, but as I made my way to the front exit, a nurse handed me a check at a reduced amount and said that they wouldn't need me in the coming weeks. They didn't tell me whether or not it was because the data my body provided didn't meet their standards, or whether they'd just rather have fewer patients exhibiting splitting headaches on the official FDA filings. But I took the money. In an e-mail after the study, Frank wrote to me that sometimes it's best not to acknowledge your symptoms if you want to collect the full amount. Frank had managed to complete the study for the full fee, and headed back down to Miami for a late summer month off.

I wondered whether I would really want to make a living testing solutions to erectile dysfunction. While the risks were likely minuscule, what was I going to get out of it other than a check and headache? And what is the purpose of having yet another Viagra knockoff on the market?

When I left my stint as a clinical laborer, I returned to the world of the uninsured and unemployed and started looking for another way to make a living. Like all lab rats, my duties were done the minute the meat of my body finished processing the drugs. I started to think about working in India. I had a master's degree. Perhaps I could run an abroad program for college students.

It turned out that I wasn't the only one looking for work abroad.

WHILE THE TESTING PROTOCOLS mean that drugs on the market are safe and vetted as thoroughly as possible, getting approval is a long and expensive process that can easily cost as much as a billion dollars. Even then, final approval is not a sure thing.

While it's true that blockbuster drugs like Viagra or an elite cancer therapy can easily offset the investment, drug developers feel pinched by the costs of drug testing in America and Europe. And yet for twenty years after the loss of prison test subjects the drug business bore the added expense. A new era dawned in the 1990s in the form of huge investments in biotech start-ups and public offerings on international stock exchanges that turned the phar-maceutical business into a high-profit/high-stakes roulette game.

Biotech companies and drug developers were increasingly led by MBA-holding boards of directors, not the scientists and clinicians who had a vested interest in patient outcomes. Speculating investors could back a company cheaply and wait for promising clinical trial results that would double a company's stock price overnight and make millions for investors even if the drug was ultimately a dud and failed during later phases of the regulatory process.

The IPO mentality meant that a drug's lifesaving properties were pegged to a bottom line. While blood-pressure regulators and treatments for hypertension and erectile dysfunction have seen a boom, others areas of research that are not as profitable have become less funded.

So many drug trials were running in the 1990s that pharmaceutical companies found themselves in over their heads and unable to cope with the load. They needed specialized help to manage the demand for drug data. Instead of doing all studies in-house and under the supervision of a university or research hospital, a slew of independent contract research organizations, or CROs, emerged that melded mercenary managerial skills with clinical sophistication. They were able to offer industrial levels of clinical testing and specialized in mass-market trials. All a scientist had to do was come up with an idea and testing protocol, and outfits like Premier Research Group in Philadelphia or Covance in Madison, Wisconsin, would run a prepackaged clinical trial off-site.

At first most contract research organizations were located in university towns where students in need of quick cash could sign up for studies. The only problem was that there weren't enough students for the number of trials. CROs began to migrate to poor areas of cities, where they could easily attract low-income residents much like the blood business did in the 1950s. Since all they were responsible for was the data, CROs could cut costs in the same way as any other corporation: by finding ever cheaper sources of labor. Today CROs dot the US-Mexico border towns, attracting migrants into the testing facilities. Between 1990 and 2001 the office of the inspector general noted that there was a sixteenfold increase of clinical trials being conducted in low-income areas. They predicted that the number would double by 2007.

The estimate proved wrong. If anything, the number of CROs active in America has actually been decreasing. The inspector general failed to account for globalization. Data collection can easily be outsourced to foreign countries with looser ethical standards, lower operating costs, and lower per-capita incomes. A 2004 study conducted by Rabo India Finance calculated that outsourcing trials to India or China would cut the overall price of a drug trial by 40 percent. By 2005 the twelve largest pharmaceutical companies conducted half of their twelve hundred clinical trials in the United Kingdom, Russia, India, and China.*

It's a fortunate situation for American drug developers, not only because they save money, but because drug trials are able to overcome the major problem with professional lab rats back home. If they set up shop in areas where patients have had little prior access to health care, they can almost guarantee that their test subjects are treatment-naive. In large part because of their governments' inability to extend health care to their citizens, both India and China have massive populations that can provide a natural human baseline of no prior treatment, even for critical conditions. By 2010 India was reaping the rewards of its overall treatment naïveté to the tune of $2 billion a year.

In India, "not only are research costs low, but there is a skilled workforce to conduct trials," says Sean Philpott, former executive editor of the *American Journal of Bioethics* and current chair

---

* Melinda Cooper, "Experimental Labour—Offshoring Clinical Trials to China," *East Asian Science, Technology and Society* 2, no. 1 (2008): 8.

of the EPA's Human Studies Review Board. The surge in willing subjects, however, raises similar questions that outlawed the prison studies in America. "Individuals who participate in Indian clinical trials usually won't be educated. Offering one hundred dollars may be undue enticement: They may not even realize that they are being coerced," he says.

The situation is similar to the pressure to sell kidneys in Tsunami Nagar. The same people who enroll in clinical trials in India belong to the same socioeconomic class as the people who are taken advantage of by kidney brokers, surrogate homes, and blood thieves. The surveillance and coercion between the markets are eerily familiar. Since the Indian Drug Control General, which plays an FDA-like role, generally has poor oversight, it is tempting for pharmaceutical companies to skirt ethical norms in order to create better data sets. There have already been mistakes.

In 2004 the Drug Control General of India investigated two high-profile biotech start-ups in Bangalore—Shantha Biotech and Biocon—for conducting an illegal clinical trial for genetically modified insulin. Eight patients died. Both companies failed to even ask for informed consent, let alone take measures to minimize the danger to patients.

In another incident, Sun Pharmaceuticals convinced four hundred doctors to prescribe Letrozole, a breast cancer drug, as a fertility treatment. They were hoping to get the drug approved for a secondary use (and double or triple sales), but failed to tell the patients they gave the drug to that they were enrolled in an experiment.

While the women reported no serious side effects, it had the potential for disaster.

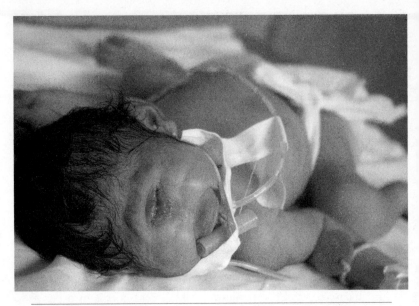

This child's birth certificate reads "Baby of Gomathi" because her family refused to name her after she was born with a severe craniofacial defect known as cyclopia. The staff of Kasturba Gandhi hospital in Chennai wrote that the rare genetic disorder could have been the result of a botched fertility treatment with the drug cyclopamine. Cyclopamine was at that time being tested in the United States as a treatment for cancer. One year before this photo was taken pharmaceutical companies tested another anticancer drug as a fertility treatment in an unregulated trial of several hundred pregnant women. While cyclopamine is available for sale in India, no company admits to testing it in India.

And it may not have been the only time that a cancer treatment was tested on women who were pregnant or hoping to get pregnant. Two years after the Letrozole trial while I was living in Chennai, I reported for *Wired News* that a child was born with severe facial distortions caused by a rare genetic disorder called cyclopia. The condition fuses the left and right hemispheres of the brain, and in this case resulted in a single eye in the center of the baby's forehead, hence the name. When I visited Kasturba Gandhi Hospital where the child was born, the staff told me that the mother had told the hospital she had been trying to get pregnant for several years and was given an unknown drug by a local fertility clinic.

In a confidential report that I was allowed to read, the hospital administration wrote that the mother may have been given an experimental anticancer drug called cyclopamine. In my research I discovered that cyclopamine was currently undergoing clinical trials in the United States. The compound, derived from the North American corn lily, had long been used by Native Americans as a contraceptive and pain reliever. In the 1950s American herdsmen noticed that pregnant goats who had been eating corn lilies gave birth to an entire generation of one-eyed kids.* Further testing of the corn lily showed that the chemical cyclopamine blocks a genetic pathway crucial to the development of the brain and prostate cancer.

Biotech giants Genentech and Cirus thought that refined cyclopamine might be able to stop prostate cancer in its tracks. Both companies denied running clinical trials in India and stated that any use of the compound on pregnant women would be dangerous. However, I was able to find drug suppliers in Mumbai and Delhi willing to sell it to me over the phone. While my follow-ups over the next few weeks provided little additional information on the case of the one-eyed baby, they raised the specter of the Letrozole experiments that had happened only a few hundred miles away.

---

* Pictures of one-eyed goats are only a Google search away.

"Third world lives are worth much less than European lives. That is what colonialism was all about," said Srirupa Prasad, a visiting professor of medical history at the University of Wisconsin–Madison.

The situation in China is potentially even more dangerous, as the government stands to make a tidy profit off the lack of medical care. The starkest examples come from Henan Province, where impoverished farmers are habitual targets for red marketers. They have both been harvested for their tissue and then used as unwitting test subjects.

Starting in the 1990s the head of Henan Provincial Department of Health set up a biotech company that paid for blood collection. The setup was similar to the days of professional donation in India, except that blood donors had no ability to bargain up the price of blood. The lab separated the blood into components and sold them on the national (and possibly international) markets. Anthropologist Ann S. Anagnost wrote that the biotech industry had transformed blood into a marketable commodity in its own right.* It is traded in a similar way to gold. Middlemen and brokers collect blood on their own and funnel it back to the cash-paying corporation without regard to how it was obtained. Anagnost writes that the military even helps to coordinate the efforts.

In a scene similar to the blood pirates in Gorakhpur, India, the only thing that mattered was the quantity of blood, not the collection processes. To save money on collection, untrained

---

* Ann S. Anagnost, "Strange Circulations: The Blood Economy in Rural China,"
  Economy and Society 35, no. 4 (November 2006): 509–29.

techs reused needles between patients and spread the HIV virus throughout the donor pools. Soon Henan had one of the highest rates of AIDS in all of China. After years of unsafe protocols, the government eventually stopped paying for blood, but the damage was already done.

In 2002, however, biotech investors turned the blood-collection-induced AIDS epidemic into an opportunity for clinical research. They began to scout through the former blood donors for test subjects on whom they could test an experimental AIDS treatment. A pilot study in 2003 conducted by California-based Viral Genetics took on thirty-four treatment-naive subjects in Henan who were in the final stages of the disease. Their condition was so far advanced that traditional antiretrovirals would not be effective. The hope was that an experimental drug called VGV-1 could restore the effectiveness of the older generation of drugs and give AIDS patients a slightly longer prognosis. They were ideal candidates because the government had never given them treatment for their HIV.

The clinical trial was the first chance that most of the former blood donors had to seek medical attention at all. When the trial started they were not offered any information about the risks or even about how the drug might help their prognosis (it wouldn't). With the help of an international network of activists the group managed to get word to the institutional review board in America responsible for green-lighting trial designs. The board responded that the trial might have needed some cosmetic changes in its informed consent policies.

But anthropologist Melinda Cooper notes that the board too narrowly focused on consent rather than on the almost systematic exploitation of people who were perennial victims of medical deceit. Never mind the contractual issues, she writes; the clinical laborers had "nothing else to sell but exposure itself."*

AT A DEEPER LEVEL, the Henan drug trial demonstrates how test subjects don't share in the benefits of pharmaceutical research. As unequal partners in drug development, they neither earn a market rate for their contributions to research, nor have access to the patented drug once it is approved.

If the new drug developed in Henan eventually led to FDA approval, then it would be highly unlikely that the drug would even be available in Chinese markets in the patients' lifetime. As with kidneys, eggs, and every other red market, the flesh of trial subjects can only move upward through the social hierarchy. Most benefits that pharmaceutical companies derive from outsourcing clinical trials are never reciprocated downward and back into the community. The poor and destitute bear the risk of testing drugs, but only the affluent receive their potential benefits. According to a 2006 study by Ernst and Young, at most only 10 percent of China's population, the percentage of people with health insurance, would ever be able to afford patented drugs.†

There's a double standard when it comes to valuing human bodies. During research people enrolled in clinical trials are altruistic volunteers helping the state of science. After the drug trial

---

* Melinda Cooper, "Experimental Labour," 16.
† This is somewhat softened by the bewildering world of international protocol and commerce, because the Chinese government generally ignores WTO demands and frequently allows domestic pharmaceutical companies to put out copyright-infringing copycat drugs.

their contributions are forgotten—participants are unable to share in either the financial rewards of a patented medication or the benefits of a new therapy. Though test subjects bear the entire physical risk in drug development, companies that go on to make billions on drug sales fail to recognize that it takes more than flesh to make a drug—it takes the minds and bodies of real people.

A three-dimensional printer at the laboratory of Organovo in California. The machine uses an ink made out of stem cells to print out human tissue. This printer could one day produce artificial organs that could be used to stop the spread of illegal markets in human tissue. However, the technology still has serious challenges to overcome.

CHAPTER NINE
IMMORTAL PROMISES

A T A FERTILITY clinic in Cyprus the rakish embryologist Savvas Koundouros waves his hand in the air as if he were erasing my questions before they even left my mouth. He is in the business of human eggs, yes, but there's a lot more to the reproduction industry than just making babies. With his voice low and heavy with cigarette smoke, he grabs my notebook and starts jotting down notes.

"The real story here is stem cells. Soon I'll have developed a new procedure to create embryonic stem cells without ever having to use a human egg." His finger, apparently restless, thrusts upward into the air as he explains that he is developing a method to create embryonic stem cells out of other tissues. One day, he says, the research will circumvent the legal ban on embryonic stem cell research in the United States that restricted scientists to just a few select lines of genetic material lucky enough to be grandfathered in before President George W. Bush banned new lines. The dearth of new material was one of the most important stumbling points for clinical progress. President Obama reversed the order in 2009, but roadblocks to the research seem to keep coming up, by way of federal court injunctions and protests by religious activists.

For decades embryonic stem cell research has been the controversial battleground in the fight between forward-thinking scientists who see stem cells as the building blocks for an extremely beneficial branch of medicine and religious groups opposed to research on embryos on the principle that it kills a potential human life. So far, the only way to develop new stem cell lines requires destroying embryos.

However, Koundouros says that his lab will be able to sidestep the religious objections and not destroy eggs at all. He will simply mature them from bone marrow or skin tissue. With the science for research purposes basically the same he would have solved a sticky political argument with a technological solution. And, he says excitedly, scientists can then get on with ushering in a new era of medicine. Perhaps with the advances laboratories might be able to regrow whole organs, repair damaged tissue, and possibly extend life forever. The potential is endless.

Soon my notebook overflows with crisscrossing lines and circles that represent eggs, strands of DNA, and the unlimited healing potential locked inside our own bodies. It takes patience and timing to finally yank the paper away from him and find some space to make my own notes on the subject. But it doesn't take long for my pen to slow down on the page and fall flat. It wasn't his fault, but I just couldn't match his enthusiasm on the subject. It was the same story I'd heard dozens of times before. Stem cells might be the future, but the hurdles to medical breakthroughs are more than simply regulatory.

We've been on the verge of a scientific revolution for decades. It seems like every few months one scientist or another predicts that in the near future like salamanders we will regrow lost limbs. Or a magazine will tout that a lab is on the verge of a breakthrough that will allow us to grow fresh and genetically perfect organs in bioreactors, or that computer technology will one day allow us to download our brains onto a hard drive to continue on in a virtual rendition of our real-life selves. Failing that, there are already companies that offer a service to cryogenically freeze our bodies so that we have a chance to wait for regenerative medicine to catch up and cure the problem of death. More than anything else, though, as a society we've pinned our hopes on various iterations of stem cell treatments to pave the way to the future of medicine.

THE WORLD FIRST HEARD about stem cells in 1963 when Ernest Armstrong McCulloch and James Till, two Toronto-based cellular scientists, showed that these root cells can transform into any other cell in the body. These so-called pluripotent stem cells could be a key to repairing or replacing any damaged human tissue. For more than a generation we have been patiently waiting for a time when our own bodies could be treated as renewable resources. Stem cells and regenerative medicine might allow us a chance to untether our inner selves, what I have called a soul, from the meat that lets us wander through the world. We're no longer stuck with the bodies that we are born with. It's immortality within reach.

Our faith in science to deliver miracle cures probably came

along in 1928 when Alexander Fleming, a Scottish pharmacologist who kept an untidy workspace, left Petri dishes of common bacteria in his lab over a long weekend. When he returned, he discovered that an opportunistic fungus had colonized and killed the bacteria—inadvertently leading to the discovery of penicillin and the first revolution of modern medicine. Within a few years hospital wards could fight off infections that had until then routinely killed people after surgery, the bubonic plague was almost completely eradicated, and killers like strep throat, tuberculosis, and syphilis were stopped in their tracks. Most of us can't remember a time when a sore throat meant all-but-certain death. But for people living at that time antibiotics were like gifts from God. Ambrosia.

Humanity's elation can be broken down into numbers. In the Middle Ages a human life span rarely exceeded twenty-five years. By 1900, a child born in the United States could expect to live about forty-seven years. A child born today should make it to the age of seventy-eight. The discovery of antibiotics along with safe blood transfusions, public health improvements, and hospital care that reduces infant mortality have added almost thirty years to life expectancies in the developed world. The eminent science writer Jonathan Weiner boils it down this way: "During the twentieth century we gained . . . about as much time as our species had gained before in the whole struggle of existence."*

In his book *Long for this World,* Weiner profiles Aubrey de Grey, a futurist and immortalist who is certain that regenerative

---

* Jonathan Weiner, *Long for This World: The Strange Science of Immortality* (New York: Ecco, 2010), 11.

medicine heralds another leap in life spans that will let us live forever. De Grey sees death as simply another medical condition begging to be solved. As medicine improves to a point where all maladies are treatable, death will merely be a problem for the uninsured.

De Grey and his disciples are outliers in the scientific community, but faith in medical science to cure our ailments is simply human. With almost a hundred years of medical miracles it is difficult to conceive that men in lab coats won't come up with consistently better treatments for our sicknesses. Where we used to pray to God for longer and healthier lives, now we pray to scientists to develop cures for the things that could kill us.

The problem with living in the age of miracle cures is that we expect them to keep coming. Sometimes small advances make the next leap forward seem tantalizingly close. Artificial versions of complex organs have been in the pipeline for more than half a century. The first artificial kidney, known now as the humble dialysis machine, was invented in 1946. The first implantation of an artificial heart in a human patient took place in 1969.

Biologically based approaches are also gaining momentum. With the help of bioreactors and hardy cell lines it is possible to grow human skin for transplants in a laboratory. Burn victims facing the prospect of harvesting skin from their own bodies for transplant have never been happier (for men, the largest swath of available skin is often the scrotum).

These modest gains are all that is keeping a nagging question at bay: What if medical science is reaching a plateau? In the twentieth century, antibiotics seemed to solve the problem of infection, however in the last thirty years resistant strains of bacteria have evolved to make most of the old first-line treatments ineffective. Staph infections caused by antibiotic-immune bacteria are quickly becoming the top killers in hospitals. Gene therapy hit a dead end when a patient died during a clinical trial. With only a few exceptions FDA-approved stem cell therapies are still decades away. In many ways, it feels like we are going back to where we started from.

As far as pharmaceutical development goes, other than antibiotics, there have been no unequivocal cures in drug development in the last century. Tested against placebos, most improvements are only fractionally more effective than therapies we had at the beginning of the twentieth century. There is no pill that can cure cancer. It takes huge regimens of debilitating drugs to maintain HIV as a chronic illness. Some drugs, like the anti-inflammatory treatment Vioxx, actually increased the chance of heart attacks and had to be recalled. Profitable antidepressants like Prozac have been linked to patient suicides and in many cases are no better at alleviating depression than plain sugar pills. Every year the FDA issues hundreds of recalls for drugs and devices that it had once approved. Despite all the activity, it isn't clear that medicine is marching forward; it might just be marching sideways.

There is one major caveat in this. While miracle cures in stem cells and drug development haven't kept pace with technical development in robotics or the Internet, revolutionary changes in surgical techniques and medical imaging come every few years. In the twentieth century the science of cutting, stitching, and rerouting different bodily systems has made the equivalent of a quantum leap.

In the 1800s surgery was a death sentence. If you didn't die from blood loss on the table, then more often than not an infection would overwhelm you during recovery. At the time the most common operations involved limb amputations. In those cases success wasn't determined as much by the skill of the surgeon or his knowledge of anatomy, but by the speed at which the doctor was able to hack through human flesh and cauterize the wound. The most famous surgeon at the time, Robert Liston, could amputate a limb in two and a half minutes.

Today operating rooms are nerve centers of high-tech innovation and, more important, success. Killers of yore—from brain aneurysms to gunshot wounds, compound fractures, heart attacks, and tumors—all stand a good chance of survival with a timely ER visit. Kidney transplants now only take a matter of hours. Hip replacements are commonplace and keyhole surgeries leave virtually no scars. We live in the golden age of the operating room.

This discrepancy between surgical innovation and stagnation in pharmaceutical development and regenerative medicine lies at the heart of the insatiable demand for human tissue in red markets around the world. Drug development and regenerative medicine have not proceeded along surgery's logarithmic curve. Drug breakthroughs have been few and far between and yet patients demand them immediately. Patients want stem cells to fix our broken kidneys and ailing hearts. Unable to find the cures they want in regenerative medicine, patients must opt for surgical fixes.

It may be every person's right to expect protection against the bubonic plague, surgery for burst appendixes, and alleviation from pain, but the issue is much more complex when treatments depend on harvesting tissue or health from another person.

. . . .

ANTHROPOLOGIST CATHERINE WALDBY, WHO coined the term *clinical labor* to describe the work of human guinea pigs, as mentioned in the clinical trials chapter, writes that markets for human tissue illustrate "the impossibility of regulating the fantasy of a regenerative body, bound up as it is with the desire for a mastery over time and fear of death, through the rationality of market forces."*

Even if the promise of regenerative medicine is technically possible in some far-flung future, there is no reason to expect it within our lifetime. In the developed world we invest great amounts of material resources, treasure, and hope into extending life a few years at a time with surgical and medicinal interventions. To some degree it even works. A new kidney can bring a person off a dialysis machine for a handful of years. The recipient of a donor heart has about a 50 percent chance of living ten more years. It's not immortality, but it's significant. Meanwhile, in many cases even if the transplant is covered by insurance or government aid, patients spend exorbitant sums of money, and even bankrupt themselves and their families paying for expensive antirejection drug regimens.

The medical industry makes it too easy to confuse buying power with a right to stave off death. Without a transplant, organ failure is a fatal condition. But rather than come to terms with the eventuality of death, entering into hospice care, and preparing loved ones for the inevitable, legal and illegal markets sell hope of more life. As I've written, a woman who is unable to conceive

---

* Catherine Waldby and Robert Mitchell, *Tissue Economies: Blood, Organs, and Cell Lines in Late Capitalism* (Durham, NC: Duke University Press, 2006), 177.

because of a medical condition can instead explore the possibility of a domestic adoption, or doctors and social workers can provide her with a wide array of medical options to bring biological offspring into the world.

If we want to live in a world where human lives are priceless and in some ways equal, then the market cannot be the best decider of which people have the right to other people's bodies. Inevitably even the best systems of tissue donation break down at some point and let in criminal elements. Even if most of the time it works without people being exploited, the crimes, when they happen, are so extreme that they undermine the benefits of the entire system to society at large.

The current ethos that rules red markets around the world is the assumption that there is an ethical way to build a commercial system of flesh exchange on top of altruistic donations. And yet the short supply of altruism around the world makes the overall system unsustainable. When that supply falters, criminal elements look for illicit ways to increase supply.

One solution to the hypocrisy would be to outlaw all monetary exchange for human tissue and bodies. This would include a ban on paying doctors for their services, tissue supply companies, medical transporters, and everyone else involved in the industry along the way. This, of course, would likely strengthen the black market and drive the industry underground while drastically reducing the supply of legal exchanges.

Alternatively, we could do away with the notion of inherent human equality and accept that the body is a commodity like any other. Embracing the market would presuppose that humans can be treated like widgets and force us to accept the inherent unfairness that some people will always supply flesh, while others will consume it. In this formulation it might be possible to regulate away the worst offenses in tissue harvesting and cut incentives to criminal brokering. And yet, what would we lose as a society by formally creating these two distinct classes of people?

In truth, these solutions are not very attractive. As a society we neither want to accept open trade in human tissue, nor do we want to reduce our access to life-extending treatments. In other words, we want to have our cake and eat it, too.

When philosophers and social scientists get to this point in the debate between a market for human tissue and the ethics of harvesting it, someone always looks for a back door and raises the possibility of a synthetic market. If technology created the ethical conundrum, perhaps it can find a way out of it as well.

"WE ARE ON THE verge of a breakthrough," says Savvas Koundouros in his breezy IVF office, confident that new stem cell therapies are just around the corner. There is no reason the revolution couldn't start here. The island of Cyprus is something of a safe haven for doctors who break the rules on the frontiers of medicine. In 1986 Koundouros's competition, Krinos Trokoudes, made the *Guinness Book of World Records* for impregnating a forty-six-year-old woman through IVF. In a more controversial case, one Cypriot doctor, Panayiotis Michael Zavos, happily proclaimed his desire to thwart the laws so he could become the first doctor to successfully clone a human. He declared 2002 "the year of human clones" and started pushing for a breakthrough in his lab. He kept the location of his office secret—ostensibly to protect the lives and identities of the offspring—and by 2009 he claimed to reporters at the *Independent* that he had tried implanting eleven cloned embryos into women ready to deliver the children. None of the embryos produced a viable offspring, but he has not indicated that he intends to stop his efforts. After all, it took 277 attempts for UK scientists to clone the sheep "Dolly." The *Independent* quoted Zavos saying that it was only a matter of time until he, or someone else, clones a human.

OUTSIDE OF THE REALM of novels like Kazuo Ishiguro's *Never Let Me Go,* in which human clones are cultivated for their replacement organs, human cloning is not going to stop the ceaseless demand for human bodies. And yet researchers around the world are searching for breakthroughs that promise to create steady supplies of artificial (and depersonalized) human tissue. A success could turn the entire world of red markets on its head.

There would be no reason to run a blood farm or steal a kidney if biologically perfect synthetic tissue and organs could be manufactured at industrial levels. No one would need a bone transplant if an injection of stem cells would grow new bone. In transplant circles people wistfully talk about how the future will be regenerative medicine. Given the complexities of the red market today, ultimately regenerative medicine might be the only sane way to unhinge the current market for human body parts and eliminate flesh-harvesting networks.

The first, and arguably most successful, case of a synthetic destroying the market for human materials occurred in 1985, when the biotech giant Genentech synthesized human growth hormone (HGH) with recombinant mRNA. Before that, injections of HGH had been shown effective in overcoming certain types of dwarfism in young children, and body builders learned that HGH could add mass to their frames and bring their muscles to new heights of definition and strength. Sure it was, and continues to be, illegal to use HGH to gain a competitive advantage, thought that hasn't stopped athletes from demanding it. But HGH wasn't easy to come by. Prior to 1985, the only way to get HGH was to harvest the pituitary glands from cadavers and almost literally squeeze out the juices from the tiny organ to extract the hormones. The process was inefficient, required a large number of glands to make a dose, and had no steady source of supply.

From the 1960s to the mid-1980s morticians and pathologists that conducted autopsies for police departments harvested hundreds of thousands of pituitaries and sold them to pharmaceutical companies who processed them into an injectable solution. It was standard practice and most people never knew that their loved ones were being cut up and sold. Still, HGH was so expensive and hard to find that hospitals had to guard their stocks tightly or thieves would steal it from their storerooms to sell on the black market.

When synthetics hit the market, the trade in pituitary glands vanished overnight. While the process to synthesize HGH isn't easy or particularly cheap, the hormone was suddenly available in much larger quantities than it had been before. It was also available without the specter and negative health side effects of injecting something that was harvested from a cadaver. While doping with HGH continues to plague the sports world, the supply chain has moved on from its roots in the flesh bazaar.

Synthetics offer hope across a spectrum of red markets. Today there are dozens—if not hundreds—of small companies investing in regenerative research that could one day pay off. By and large they fall into two distinct camps: First are laboratories exploring ways to stimulate the body's own ability to cure itself by either providing cellular raw materials that can cure broken or aging parts, or unlocking hidden genetic codes that will activate dormant curative properties. Researchers in this vein assume that the body already knows how to cure its problems, and just needs a little help to finish the job. This includes the world of stem cell therapies, gene therapies that unlock regenerative potential, and almost the entire field of alternative medicine.

The second school of regenerative medicine is often agnostic on the subject of self-regeneration, but assumes that with enough data, we can use our technical know-how to fix any bodily problem. Replacement bodies can be built from the ground up and surgically manipulated to function. This is the realm of prosthetic and robotic limbs, synthetic tissue and organs, and artificial hormones.

Both schools of thought have made basic advances that have kindled the hope of millions of patients. And yet the research prognosis is so far out that neither is likely to turn off the demand for human tissues any time soon.

For example, take stem cells and any one of the hundreds of anecdotal miracle events that happen, and get reported on, every year.

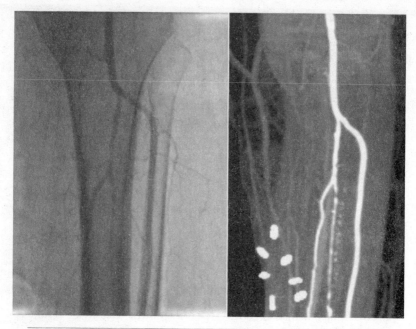

Vamal Cattacha's angiogram shows veins in her leg after an experimental stem cell treatment in Chennai, India. The image shows that new veins have grown in as bright white streaks. If the treatment had not been successful, doctors would have had to amputate her leg. The success has not been duplicated since.

In 2006 a seventy-year-old diabetes patient named Vamal Cattacha was reclining in a hospital bed on an airy medical ward in Chennai. She smiled when I entered the room with S. R. Subrammaniyan, a doctor who was wearing a blue button-down shirt and a pressed white lab coat. Without his help, Cattacha was sure that she would never walk again, and I had come along to document her recovery. Earlier that year she noticed a small pinprick-sized cut on her leg, but assumed it would go away. After a few weeks of not paying attention, it had spread into a twenty-two-inch-long gaping ulcer that stretched from the heel of her foot to her mid-calf.

Leg ulcers like hers are common among diabetes patients. As the disease progresses, veins and arteries in the limbs start to atrophy and disappear, making it hard to recover from seemingly insignificant injuries. Small wounds can lead to big problems and often leave people permanently disabled. According to the American Diabetes Association, ulcers like Cattacha's are responsible for almost 60 percent of nontraumatic amputations in American hospitals. That's roughly eighty-two thousand amputations a year in the United States. While there is no official number of amputations in India, diabetes rates are even higher on the subcontinent than in the United States.

Cattacha, however, wasn't willing to take amputation for an answer. She traveled across South India looking for a doctor who could give her any other options. Even a sliver of hope would do. Eventually she met Subrammaniyan, who had recently partnered with a Japanese stem cell company that wanted to test a new breed of regenerative therapies. Other than the gaping wound on her leg, Cattacha was in pretty good health, which made her a good candidate for an experiment.

The plan was deceptively simple. Subrammaniyan drew adult stem-cell-rich bone marrow from Cattacha's hip and then separated the stem cells from the normal blood cells with a centrifuge. Over the next week he injected a solution that he made out of the stem cells into her leg and grafted a piece of skin over the wound.

Within sixty days, the ulcer had visibly healed, and bright white signatures of arteries streaked across her post-treatment angiograms. Before the injections her leg had had almost no circulation at all. The stem cells had apparently re-formed significant lengths of her atrophied circulatory system.

Subrammaniyan called the media, and soon local papers were extolling the virtues of the out-of-the-way medical center. And yet despite the success, the doctor's explanation was enigmatic. "No one quite knows how it works," said Subrammaniyan, "but somehow, once injected, the stem cells know how to transform into the right sort of cells."

For Cattacha the pain was gone, but an isolated success story is not a revolution in stem cell treatment. When I originally reported on the treatment for *Wired News,* doctors in the United States cautioned against reading too much into the results.

"This was a single case with no controls," wrote Geoffrey Gurtner, associate professor of surgery at Stanford University and an expert on diabetes care, in an e-mail. "We know that in any disease state, some patients get better even in the absence of care for reasons we do not entirely understand."

Over the next three years, while I was living a half mile from the hospital, I checked in with the doctors to see if they were ever able to replicate the success, or at least give a more definitive explanation of Cattacha's recovery. There was never any real news. They continued to test stem cell treatments on humans— occasionally issuing press releases about paralyzed patients who regained partial movement after an injection similar to Cattacha's. In every other case I checked into, what appeared to be a miracle ended up not being repeatable, the results ambiguous.

The underlying problem is that for the most part no one really understands how stem cells work in a therapeutic setting. The theory is that the body knows how to heal itself and that stem cells somehow know where they are most needed in the body and then set about fixing the problem on their own. For the most part researchers see their own role in therapy as delivery agents.

And yet the appeal of the experiment is obvious. With no reliable therapies, a person who has been injured in a traumatic accident, or is suffering from a broken spine or failing organs, doesn't have much to lose. Is it better to pursue a path of slim hope with doctors who will experiment on their bodies, or feel helpless and trapped in a world of no good options?

IN NEW DELHI, JUST three hours north of Chennai by plane, Geeta Shroff is a pioneering doctor in experimental stem cell therapy on humans. She's not so concerned about understanding the exact mechanisms of stem cells as she is about trying new methods and hoping for results. She's a doctor of last resort for people who have gone everywhere else. In her lab she enthusiastically injects her own embryonic stem cell brew into a stream of patients from around the world, treating broken spinal cords, progressive neurological diseases, and terminally ill people at a cost of $20,000 to $30,000 per treatment.

With the shadow of regulators bearing down on them, few scientists in the Western world would rush to treat patients with experimental stem cell cocktails without first going through years of animal and toxicity trials. But in India the lack of regulation gives Shroff's research design a modicum of freedom. And the clinical trial industry is flourishing. Patients swear that Shroff has unlocked the stem cell secret. But she doesn't let many people see the inside of her lab, and has never said a word about her failure rate.

There's just no way to know whether she is a hack or a vanguard. Without publishing a paper about her results, her lab gains notoriety through the anecdotes of spectacular success. And yet no respected scientist has been able to scrutinize her methods. Mridu Khullar, a journalist in Delhi who has followed Shroff's work, had a rare and exclusive look at the lab and wrote about the story of a twenty-seven-year-old American woman who was admitted to the clinic in 2009 while suffering from chronic Lyme disease. When the patient returned home her consulting physician declared her asymptomatic. In her article, Khullar suggested that Shroff wants to eventually distribute her cure to pharmacies, saying that her treatment could be the new penicillin: "That was the beginning of the antibiotic era, and it changed the entire face of infection around the world. This is similar to that," she writes, quoting Shroff.

The risks, of course, are huge. Left to their own devices, stem cells in the bloodstream could either be therapeutic and fix a problem, or they could morph into just about any other cellular structure. One of the most serious would be to transform into a teratoma, which is a sort of tumor that mutates freely. They're best known for sometimes packing bits of bone and teeth inside of them. A poorly placed teratoma in the body can be fatal.

And without truly understanding how stem cells work—and under what conditions they transform into helpful structures or spread uncontrollably—testing on humans is risky. It could be that every injection of Shroff's cocktail is a game of Russian roulette, with results that are similar to getting blood transfusions without understanding the difference between blood types. Sometimes it could be fatal. Sometimes it could save a life.

ATTEMPTING TO MITIGATE THE risk that comes with unpredictability, a company in San Diego controls exactly where stem cells go in the body by placing them individually in a scaffold. Building on the idea that it is possible to collect enough data on human physiology, it hopes to be able to create replacement body parts from scratch. Located in a small office complex that resembles a suburban strip mall, Organovo is a tiny biotech company that uses a three-dimensional printer to build replacement organs and tissues that will one day be surgically implanted into patients.

Keith Murphy, the company's CEO, has a background at MIT as well as a degree in business. He says that most of the industry has gotten stem cell treatments backward. "The problem is that they want to inject stem cells and let them go to work on their own. But if the cells enter the blood stream most of those cells float freely around the body. No one knows where they go." Even if it isn't dangerous, it's not surprising, he says, that so few doctors have shown any sort of clinical results in a lab if the medicine isn't reaching the areas they want it to.

Murphy believes that stem cells respond to their environment and can form into just about any organic structure as long as they are getting the proper cues. In 2007 a Missouri-based partner of his firm demonstrated that beating heart cells would beat in unison when placed in a line together. The finding demonstrated that cells could communicate with their neighbors in an artificial setting—a prerequisite for printing out an artificial beating heart.

At the moment though, the organ-printing business is taking baby steps.

Murphy has me don a set of medical scrubs, shoe covers, a face mask, and hair covering and then leads me back into the sterile room. A team of three technicians huddle over a long metal device that moves a shuttle back and forth over a cell culture like an ink-jet printer. In fact that is exactly what it is, a 3-D printer that lays cells into molds—eventually forming replacement veins and arteries. On the day I visit, a thin white streak barely wider than a single angel-hair noodle is suspended between two calipers in a refrigerator next to the printer. The small bit of tissue is still maturing, but in a few days the cells will have grown out of the scaffolding laid during the printing and bond together. Eventually it will be able to hold the equivalent of human blood pressure and be ready for transplant.

The people who designed the organ printer look at the body in the same way as a mason looks at a brick building. A human organism is incredibly complex and interrelated, but ultimately we are just a bunch of cells placed one on top of the other. If there were a detailed enough diagram that noted the position and type of every cell, then a sophisticated machine could simply build a new human. Or, more realistically, print out human spare parts as they are needed.

The process starts with a culture of cellular material harvested from the intended recipient. Most likely this means an extract of bone marrow, or perhaps a biopsy from a liver. Those cells are then grown in a lab until they reach enough mass that they can be molded into inklike dollops of printable cells. The printer then positions each cell along a preset pattern to create tissues and organs. In 2010 Organovo started animal trials with nerve cells and arteries, and hopes to move on to human trials in the near future.

Organ printing seems to have some clear advantages over stem cell therapeutics, but it is still decades away from delivering real success. Its most difficult stumbling block is managing the different cell types that exist in every part of the body. Murphy points to the artificial blood vessel that will one day make its way into a mouse. "I could print you out a cube of liver cells tomorrow, but so far we haven't been able to create the blood vessels that are inside the liver at the same time as we print the liver cells." Without a steady flow of nutrients the cells in the middle of the block die. The current technology takes a few days for the cells in a vascular system to set and be able to handle human blood pressure. Pumping in fluids before that would cause the tiny constructs to burst apart.

He says the main problem now is overcoming the technical obstacles of maturing a diversity of cell types inside a complete piece of synthetic flesh.

"The only thing holding us back is investment. If the government decided that this was a priority, it would only be a matter of years before this technology matures," says Murphy when I ask how likely it would be that the company overcomes the challenges in front of it.

Organovo is in a similar position to its counterparts in India. The technology points to a possible solution to a persistent problem, but is still a long way from proving its efficacy as a viable treatment. When Organovo first appeared on the scene, media outlets across the Internet predicted that the age of replacement organs was just around the corner. However the science is still far behind the expectations we have placed on it. Murphy is hesitant to suggest that even with massive amounts of funding a working artificial organ is any less than ten years away. More than likely we will have to wait a lot longer than that.

Synthetic replacement tissues, miracle therapies, and immortal cell lines may one day be the key to fixing the problem with the global tissue shortage. Industrial production facilities could one day replace red markets that are built on harvesting human bodies to prolong lives. We all want to believe in stories where ingenious scientist entrepreneurs save the day and create alternatives to solve the problems of today. But what are the costs of putting our hopes in the fringes of science fiction before they are science facts? Today there is already an economic system that provides vast amounts of human materials for sick people who can pay for it. We already treat human tissue as if the only problem is acquiring the raw materials.

At the heart of every red market is a kernel of hope that a bit of matter harvested from another human will in some way make the recipient's life better. In some cases it does. However, the question of supply waits patiently in the background as if it is just another technicality that can be easily overcome. There is little will to change the current situation because we all believe the ethical conundrums of today will soon seem like anachronisms from a distant past. Rather than live our lives in an uncertain future, perhaps it is best to explore what is really happening along red market supply chains.

.   .   .   .

BACK IN CYPRUS I watch Savvas Koundouros pull out his fifth cigarette from a crumpled pack and suck in deeply. We are on the roof of the building; a small refrigerator that keeps some of his less critical biological materials, and for which there is no space in the office, hums along next to him. Somewhere inside his lab another cryogenic storage locker holds hundreds of fertilized embryos awaiting their opportunity for him to implant the genetic bundle into another woman's ovaries.

"Yes." He nods. "Stem cells are the future." But for now, at least, he is in the business of harvesting and selling embryos to women who can pay for them.

Hair harvested from the heads of Hindu devotees in Tirupati, India, dries on a rack in Chennai. These bunches will eventually make their way to the United States and Europe and be transformed into wigs and hair weaves.

CHAPTER TEN
BLACK GOLD

A N ATTENDANT PEEPING out of an old-fashioned bank-teller window stashes my shoes in a giant pile with a thousand other pairs. From here there is no way out. A ripe throng of humanity presses me through a series of wrought-iron gates, and I trip along crumbling bits of concrete. As we make the transition from the entranceway to the inner sanctum, cool white ceramic tiles replace the broken flooring. It takes fifteen minutes to inch my way forward through the herd of people pressed together like cattle to where a uniformed man in a booth hands me a paper token imprinted with a bar code and a picture of Venkateswara— an incarnation of the Hindu god Vishnu. The next official I meet a few feet away, clad in a stained brown shirt, hands over two razor blades: one for my head, the other for my face.

The crowd of men and women proceed down a wide stair-case, whose landing is covered in a soggy mixture of tepid water and black hairballs. The air is moist and smells of rancid coconut oil. The stairs end at a vast, tiled chamber resembling a neglected Olympic swimming facility where long lines of men face tiled benches running along the walls. (Women are herded into a separate room.) In the center are four massive steel vats.

I match my token code—MH1293—to a sign on the wall and then take my place in a queue of about fifty bare-chested men in black sarongs. The pilgrim at the head of the line bows low as a man with a straight razor makes swift work of his curls. Satisfied, the barber looks up, spots me, and beckons me forward. He has a ragged cloth tied around his waist over white striped boxer shorts. No high priest, clearly. Just a worker bee for the holy hive.

I assume the position as he fixes my blades to the razor handle. "Start praying," he says. I try to remember the god's face, but there's no time to contemplate: the man forces my head downward and runs the blade down from the top of my head with the practiced efficiency of a sheepherder. Satisfied, he grabs my chin, sticking a thumb in my mouth as he prepares to dispense with my beard. I watch the brown hair fall away in clumps, joining the dark, wet mash underfoot.

The curly-haired guy who was ahead of me is also now bald, with small nicks in his scalp and pink streaks of blood dripping down his back. He meets my eyes and smiles broadly.

"Venkateswara will be pleased." His wife is offering her hair in the other room. Together they will return to their village bearing a symbol of humility and devotion that all will recognize. A woman in a blue sari flashes by and scoops my hair from the gutter into a bucket. Each time her bucket fills, she stands on her tiptoes and empties it into one of the tall vats. By day's end all four will be filled with hair destined for the auction block.

Welcome to the Kalyana Katta hair-tonsuring center at the Sri Tirumula Temple in Andhra Pradesh, India: the genesis point for the world's most lucrative trade in human detritus. Hair collected here feeds into a half-billion-dollar beauty industry that weaves real "premium grade" Indian hair onto the heads of mostly African American women who want long straight hair. The global market for human hair tops out at almost $900 million in sales, and that doesn't include the installation costs that salons charge.

Women seeking a high-end look know what to ask for. It's called "remy" hair, which is more or less synonymous with hair from India. Top salons prize it for the way it's collected, in a single cut, which preserves the orientation of the hair's shinglelike outer layer, and thus its strength, luster, and feel. That's what defines remy, and that's the reason it commands a premium price. The hair's journey, shorn from the heads of the devout and sewn onto the skulls of America's new glamouratti, is a red market supply chain unlike any other. That's because in this case at least, altruism, transparency, and commercialism are perfectly balanced so that there's no black market to speak of.

Name-dropped in the ancient Hindu epic the *Mahabharata*, Tirumala is holy ground for fifty thousand annual pilgrims who arrive daily from across South Asia to seek favors from their god. In addition to monetary donations, about one in four offer their hair, which will then be offered to the gods of the marketplace, reaping a reported $10 million to $15 million each year. Including donations, the temple boasts that it takes in more money than the Vatican—a dubious claim. In any case, temple leaders announced a plan to plate the walls of the inner sanctum with gold. Profits from the hair are used to support temple programs and feed the needy.

Indian hair is sold to two distinct markets. The bulk of it, some five hundred tons per year from short-haired men like me, is purchased by chemical companies that use it to make fertilizer or L-cystine, an amino acid that gives hair its strength, but also makes an excellent additive for baked goods and other products. The more lucrative hair of female pilgrims—temple employees call it "black gold"—is tied in individual bundles and brought to the tonsuring center's top floor, where women in cheap flower-print saris labor over small heaps of the stuff, sorting it by length. An armed guard frisks all who exit. There's no way anyone is going to get past him with a single precious strand.

Human hair contains all sorts of secretions, including sweat and blood, plus food particles, lice, and the coconut oil many Indians use as a conditioner. Put twenty-one tons of the stuff in a room blooming with mildew and fungus and the stench is overpowering. One volunteer, her own long hair bound in a tight braid, appears to smile at me, but she's wearing a scrap of cloth over her nose and mouth, so she might be grimacing. As the women work I watch as lumps of the black mass seem to jump and writhe on their own—suddenly a rat almost a foot long scurries out of the jumble and races across the room into a pile of canvas bags. It's difficult to imagine that bits of this foul-smelling heap may one day adorn the heads of American pop stars.

The reincarnation of temple hair as a beauty accessory started out as a relatively humble affair. Until the early 1960s, the temple simply burned the hair it collected. Citing pollution, the government banned the practice during the 1990s, but by then the temple had already found a more profitable way to get rid of the waste. Wig makers began seeking raw materials at Tirumala. At the temple's first auction, in 1962, the hair sold for ₹16 a kilo—about $24.50 in today's dollars. Now it fetches up to ten times as much, and the auctions have become cutthroat affairs.

To see for myself, I drive a few miles to the bustling town of Tirupati, where the temple's marketing unit operates out of a string of warehouses filled with drying hair. In a large board-room, Indian traders representing forty-four companies are crowded around tables, prepared to drop millions of dollars in a complicated process of backroom negotiations. "The hair busi-ness is unlike any other," says Vijay, who owns a hair-exporting house called Shabanesa, and like many South Indians goes by a single name. "In any other business, buying a commodity is easy; it's the selling it to retailers that is difficult. Here it's all reversed. It's simple to sell hair, just difficult to buy it."

In a sense the Indian hair trade resembles other red markets in that the human materials are difficult to harvest and overall a scarce resource. Men and women who give up their hair do so in the name of God. While the temple has constructed several buildings to accommodate the thousands of people who come to offer up their hair every day, it doesn't advertise to its flock to fur-ther profit from an engorged supply. Unlike other red markets, however, human hair is ultimately a waste product, and the recent trade in it created its market value. (The same could be said about other body parts. Before medical technology allowed for kidney transplants there was simply no market.)

Which is why when sold in bulk, hair is the only human tis-sue that can be treated like an ordinary commodity, bought and sold by the pound instead of as a specific entity with an important biological history. It's the only case of pure altruism actually working in a market for human materials. But that doesn't mean hair sellers don't squabble over the profits.

I can see the tensions at the auction. The temple is pressing for a better price than last year's, and traders are worried that the global economic meltdown will batter the extensions market. Halfway through the evening India's largest hair reseller—K. K. Gupta, whose Gupta Enterprises did a brisk $49 million in sales in 2008—accuses the temple directors of trying to set an inflated price and walks out. After an hour, which Gupta spends in the parking lot making calls and threatening to go to the papers, the price is set slightly lower. Then another reseller loudly charges that Gupta is trying to corner the market. A muscular bidder has to step in to prevent fisticuffs.

Another three hours and it's approaching midnight. The price for the longest and most durable product hovers around $193 per kilo ($70 less than the previous year, I'm told). Over the next few days trucks will deliver the hair to the distributors' factories, where the alchemy of transforming human waste into a luxury product takes place.

SOME EIGHTY-FIVE MILES FROM the auction site, in an industrial lot on the outskirts of the coastal metropolis of Chennai, George Cherian, chairman of Raj Impex, one of India's largest hair-export houses, awaits his delivery. The hair must be checked for lice, painstakingly untangled, washed in vats of detergent, and combed until it's of export quality. "The real value of what we do is right here, when we grade the hair and transform it from waste into something beautiful," Cherian says. He pulls out a handful of smoothed hair the size of a riding crop, noting that it will fetch $15 on the international market.

The bulk of hair sold in India isn't tonsured, he notes—it comes from garbage bins, the floors of barber shops, and the combs of long-haired women. Nomadic families and small businesses go door-to-door bartering hair clips, rubber bands, and trinkets for it. "This work supports tens of thousands of people across India in cottage sorting and collecting industries," Cherian says. "The rule is simple: Remy hair goes to the US, the rest goes to Africa."

In a storage room, he shows me 400 kilos of remy hair packed in boxes and bound for cities throughout the world. His warehouse contains several tons more, ready to ship. "The demand is huge," Cherian says, "but I don't think that anyone outside of India would ever be able to do this. We survive because of the cheap labor. No one in Italy, or California, could prepare the hair for less."

When I asked him about the nonremy industry Cherian suggests that I contact a band of gypsies who live by the railroad tracks north of Chennai. He tells me though that I'll have to leave early if I want to catch them.

At eight in the morning I'm behind the wheel of a black Hyundai Santro dashing north through the city's narrow streets. Beside me is one of Cherian's agents, named Damodharan, who relays with gypsies and buys their product in bulk. He points me down a dirt road offshoot near a former colony for railroad workers and we turn into what looks like a barren field. But as I look closer I can make out a group of people squatting in the shadows over a small open fire. Damodharan jumps out and pulls me over to meet Raj, a slender twenty-something man with a thick crop of

black hair on his head. When I tell him I'm interested in knowing about hair selling, he smiles broadly and walks back to his
encampment and fishes around inside a large pipe that looks like
it is there to drain runoff. Then, with a flourish, he pulls out a
giant plastic bag and brings it to me.

I look over curiously and he reveals a pillow-sized greasy
black hairball. "You can find hair almost anywhere," he says. In
the mornings he shoulders a large canvas sack on his back and
trolls the side streets looking in trash cans and along roadsides.
"People just throw it out, or sometimes if they save it up for us we
will trade them," he says. Damodharan gives Raj ₹800 ($20) for
the full sack of cast-off nonremy hair that he has collected.

Back at the Raj Impex factory, workers will comb out literally
thousands of similar dreaded hair balls. Once the hair is separated,
workers will bundle it into batches and sew it onto cloth strips.
Processing nonremy hair is extremely labor-intensive, but only
about a third as lucrative. If it's long enough it goes into budget-
priced wigs. Otherwise it is transformed into mattress stuffing or
boiled down into food additives. Still, with hundreds of thousands
of tons of it available, the hair resellers can find a way to profit
from it. Like any other commodities market, plentiful supply of
cheap hair means that someone will find a way to make use of it
and spur demand somewhere.

From Chennai the best quality hair travels to almost every
beauty parlor and hair salon on the planet, but, as mentioned earlier, finds its most profitable reception in predominantly African
American neighborhoods where customers value Indian hair for
its dark, luxurious hues and straightness. One of those places,
the Grooming Room on Brooklyn's Nostrand Avenue, a street so

densely packed with beauty outlets that it almost seems zoned for that purpose, is managed by Tiffany Brown, a high priestess of hairstyles. When I first meet her on a Friday, her face is framed by closely cropped bangs and long tresses that hang to her chin. On Saturday she looks altogether different, with hair pulled tight against her scalp into a ponytail just an inch long. By Sunday she might well wear glamorous locks cascading down her back. The secret of Brown's chameleon powers: remy hair from factories like Raj Impex.

It's "a necessary accessory, like earrings or a necklace," she says. "It lets me be whoever I want to be for a day." Her clients feel the same way; they spend about $400 a month maintaining their extensions, she says, though a few drop thousands. Between shops like hers and celebs who might shell out $10,000 or more for a single wig or weave, there is a near-constant demand for Indian locks. "If you want cheap hair," sniffs a supplier's blog called thelookhairandmakeup.com, "you're going to get a cheap-looking hairstyle."

"The only hair worth buying is remy," says one of Brown's clients, her hair wrapped around enormous curlers. "They say that it's cut from the heads of virgins." Though not strictly true, the hair woven onto her head went from being an act of humility and altruism in the name of God, to one of America's most recognizable glamour enhancers.

The original caption for this photo read, "Material for anatomy studies is plentiful at a cemetery where many old bones have been unearthed. Student is Loretta Hardesty of Butte, Montana." The image ran in the January 4, 1947, issue of *Life* magazine. *(Courtesy of the Estate of Juan Guzman)*

ODE TO LORETTA HARDESTY

TOWARD THE END of 1946 a twenty-something woman in an ankle-length skirt and a white shirt embroidered with brightly colored flowers painted on a canvas and easel in a cemetery in San Miguel de Allende, Mexico. Dilapidated wooden crosses, now little more than rotten planks, jutted out of the loose dirt at odd angles, and piles of discarded bones lay on the ground. Femurs, ribs, and skulls without teeth poked out of the loose soil and mixed together pell-mell so that it was impossible to tell which bones belonged to which bodies. Two young boys watched the woman spread charcoal onto a canvas as she sketched the gruesome scene. Originally from Butte, Montana, Loretta Hardesty traveled south of the American border to study art at the Escuela Universitaria de Bellas Artes.

A few feet away a German-born photographer who had fled persecution back home and Mexicanized his name to Juan Guzman focused his lens on the scene and shot a series of pictures. One of them ran in the January 4, 1947, issue of *Life* magazine.

The article was such a smashing success that the school, which at the time had only fifty American students, received more than six thousand applications for the next year. The piece appealed to a new generation of American GIs who thought that living cheaply and painting skulls and nudes in Mexico would be a lot more pleasant than scraping a living together back home. It was the first time ever that the school had to turn away applications.

The art school needed at least two types of bodies. It needed living students who could pay first-world money for tuition, and the dead bodies of locals who unwittingly provided raw materials for anatomical sketching. The photo in *Life* is striking not because it depicts a horrible crime, but rather because of the juxtaposition of a pretty young woman in a field of scattered bones. For an art student, it didn't matter how the bones left their grave, only that they were good subjects for anatomical studies. The image is a microcosm of every red market that ever existed. Both Guzman and Hardesty are passive observers of a supply chain that begins with human tragedy.

When I look at the photo I wonder what Mohammed Mullah Box, the cemetery caretaker I met outside of Kolkata, would think if he saw it. Every night he checks his village's graveyard and wonders if it will be safe for him to leave the bodies unguarded, or if he should spend the night awake listening for the sound of shovels. He knows that it is only a matter of time until they strike again, and that there is little he can do with his bamboo cane to stop them. For the villagers of Harbati, there is nothing neutral about grave robbery.

After almost four years studying the breadth of red markets, I am no longer shocked by the gory details of an autopsy or the depth to which a criminal will sink to harvest human materials. Rather, I am only surprised at how normal it is to simply shrug our shoulders and take the supply chain for granted.

For the most part we are comfortable with the idea of buying bodies and body parts as long as we don't really know where they come from. Ideally we would buy human kidneys like we would any other meat in the grocery store: wrapped in plastic and Styrofoam with no hint of the slaughterhouse. At some level we all know that it took a sacrifice to bring a human body to the market, but we just don't want too many details.

Most of us know someone whose life has been saved by an emergency blood transfusion, or a family who has adopted a child from a foreign country. We have probably met people who have benefited from fertility treatments, or who have had their lives extended by an organ transplant. We certainly know doctors who have studied anatomy on real human skeletons; and we have taken drugs that were first tested on human guinea pigs.

It is not bad that these things exist. Some of the most important advances in science have only been made possible precisely because we have treated people as things. Who we are as people depends a lot on who we are as meat. And for the most part we do okay managing the difficult terrain between our physical selves and the part of us that, for lack of a better concept, has a soul.

Criminal and unethical red markets are far smaller than their legitimate counterparts. According to the World Health Organization, about 10 percent of world organ transplants are obtained on the black market. As a rule of thumb, that figure seems to apply to just about every other market for human bodies as well.

The stakes are high. Who we are as a society depends on how we address that remaining 10 percent. Do we let blood brokers and child kidnappers ply their trade and write off the human fall-out as just another cost of doing business? The prevalence of kidney brokers in the third world and exploited Eastern European egg sellers in the former Soviet bloc has as much to do with global economic inequalities as it does with the way we manage red markets. Is it even possible to set up a system that minimizes damage across all red markets?

Reducing the number of criminals is not only a legal problem; the solution must come from a fundamental reevaluation of our long-held beliefs on the sanctity of the human body, economics, altruism, and privacy. We need to stop viewing the demand for bodies and human tissue as a fixed issue that can only be answered by increasing the overall supply. Instead, the demand for organs, hair, children, and bones is first and foremost a function of overall (and perceived) supply. If bones are freely available in Asia, someone will find a way to make use of them. If more kidneys enter into the market, doctors will deem more people eligible for kidney transplants. The more adoption agencies advertise overcrowded orphanages, the more people will come forward to take the children into their homes. And the more eggs available on the open market, the more people will fly to other countries to receive them.

Demand on its own is meaningless. Just because there is high demand for hot rod cars, atomic bombs, first-edition *Spiderman* comics, and Rolex watches does not mean that we can or should ramp up production across the board. Without supply, that demand carries no weight.

Take the demand for blood. While high stocks of blood in the first half of the last century meant surgeons could develop vastly improved surgical techniques, certain religious groups—most notably Christian Scientists—were opposed to any sort of blood transfusion. Over the years the complete lack of demand for human blood among these people led to private investment and eventually to great strides forward in the field of bloodless surgeries. At first doctors wasted blood in order to gain more surgical sophistication; however, when they could not extend the benefits of routine procedures to everyone, the prohibition of blood use created a boom in technologies that reduced blood loss during surgeries across the board.

Today, in hospitals in the United States and Europe with access to advanced technologies, many types of operating room procedures use little or no blood at all. Though the science has a ways to go, one day the same could be true in the case of artificial organs that could make living transplants irrelevant.

Even more important, it is impossible to build an economic system that depends on altruism as a source of raw materials. In an ideal world no one would buy or sell another human being—all exchanges of humanity would be based on reciprocity and goodwill to all. That world, however, is not the one we live in. Very few people give away their kidney or eggs, or risk their health in a clinical trial out of pure goodwill. While I do not believe that commercial transactions for human tissue will curtail the existence of black markets, clearly the hypocrisy of using altruism as an excuse to buy cheap raw materials does nothing to serve the greater good. The meager payments granted to the people who sell their bodies merely puts the pressure of selling flesh on people lower down on the social totem pole.

In the case of international adoption, altruism sometimes serves an even more perverse end. Instead of helping out children already stuck in orphanages, a few corrupt agencies are able to use adoption fees meant to support charity work to fund criminal enterprises.

Although it sounds good on paper and on the floor of Congress, altruism is simply not a reliable foundation for collecting and distributing human bodies. At its best it diminishes the incentive for people to supply red markets, and at its worst altruism is a convenient cover story for taking advantage of donors.

Finally, red markets will flourish as long as legal markets in bodies are not transparent. The condition for any ethical human body or tissue exchange depends on absolute transparency of the supply chain.

Even in the best hospitals in the United States, it is almost impossible to know the identity of a brain-dead donor who gave up his or her organs so that another person could live. Most adoption agencies prefer to keep the identities of the birth parents secret to protect them from uncomfortable questions down the line, and nurses and doctors routinely scrub the names of egg donors off the official paperwork. While the intentions are usually noble, it is far too easy for unethical practitioners to harvest organs from unwilling donors, kidnap children and sell them into the adoption stream, steal blood from prisoners, and coerce women into selling eggs under dangerous conditions. In every case criminals can use the guise of privacy to protect their illicit supply chains.

The depersonalization of human tissue is one of the broadest failings of modern medicine. Our goal in this century should be to integrate and repersonalize human identities into the supply chain. Every bag of blood should include the name of the original donor, every adopted child should have full access to their personal history, and every transplant recipient should know who gave an organ.

This would require a major change in the way we think about the use and reuse of human bodies. Every human has a history that needs to be told as his or her body moves through a red market. We aren't born as neutral products that are by nature reducible to commercial barter. But undoubtedly we all are customers on a red market. The sooner we accept that, the sooner we can do something about it.

And so the same standards that apply to buying used cars should also apply to buying body parts. It isn't legal to sell stolen cars, nor is it legal to sell ones that are sure to break down. Savvy customers always get accident reports before they invest money in a used vehicle. If cars have histories, then so should bodies. Why shouldn't parents be able to check to see if it is possible to locate the parents of the child that they adopted, or someone who bought an egg for implantation check to have access to the medical history of the donor's family? Shouldn't we know whose skeleton hangs in our doctor's closet?

Transparency won't solve every problem. Undoubtedly criminals will be able to forge paperwork, invent new backstories, and disguise unethical practices in new and imaginative ways. International boundaries and changes in legal jurisdictions make it easier for criminals to hide their tracks. However, a clear paper trail makes it easier to flag dangerous operators.

In 1946 Loretta Hardesty calmly painted the dismembered bodies of Mexican peasants without worrying much about how the bones found their way out of their graves. More than sixty years later I hope we're able to ask the questions that she did not.

ACKNOWLEDGMENTS

I BELIEVE THAT writers are only as good as their editors. I have been fortunate enough to work with some of the most talented wordsmiths in the industry, who have labored over my half-formed ideas and counseled me through challenging and occasionally dangerous assignments. This book would simply not have been possible without Matthew Benjamin at William Morrow, who saw this project from its infancy. My mentor and confidant, Ted Greenwald, who, as senior editor at *Wired,* introduced me to feature writing and showed me that a career in journalism was possible. With steady hands and swift guidance, Mike Mechanic and Monika Bauerlein at *Mother Jones* helped see three chapters of this book to completion. Also Bill Leuders, Sarah Spivack, and Jeff Chu played a hand in helping refine my ideas.

Rachel Swaby, Sonja Sharp, and Jennifer Phillips, who comprise the fact-checking teams at *Wired* and *Mother Jones,* helped to ensure the accuracy of almost everything in this book, sometimes going so far as to reverse-report entire features, listening to count-less hours of tape to confirm the direct quotes in much of this manuscript.

Some of the most difficult research subjects were made eas-ier with the help of excellent on-the-ground assistants in India, Cyprus, and Spain. Divya Trivedi has accompanied me on assign-ments in four states across North India, from blood farms and surrogate clinics to police stations and militant camps. In Chen-nai, Hassan Mohammed and Sripriya Somashekhar translated interviews with kidney sellers and brokers. In West Bengal, Arup Gosh led me though a netherworld of bone dealers and grave robbers. In Spain and Cyprus, Rabia Williams, Lucas Psillakis, and Christina Boudylina helped inquire into the dark side of the human egg business.

Between 2006 and 2010 my work has been generously sup-ported by the Fund for Investigative Journalism and the Pulit-zer Center on Crisis Reporting as well as a short residency at the Ledig House Writers Retreat in Omi, New York.

The credit for this book's being published at all goes largely to my former literary agent, Mary Ann Naples, of the Creative Cul-ture, who graciously told me which ideas were worth pursing and which were best relegated to the dustbin of nonfiction literature. She started a new career online, but left me in the capable hands of Laura Nolan, at DeFiore and Company, who has stewarded my work to completion. I look forward to a long relationship with her.

Of course many other people along the way offered advice and opened doors that might otherwise have been closed. In no particular order I'd like to thank Jaya Menon, Neha Dixit, Bappa Majumdar, David Sher, Catherine Waldby, Stefanos Evripidou,

Rama Rau, Doros Polycarpou, Arun Dohle, Mags Gavan, Joost Van der Valk, Tim Perell, Jason Miklian, Tom Pietrasik, John Wheeler-Rappe, Danielle Anastasion, Anne Yang, Wen-yi, Lisa Ling, Raymond Telles, Marshall Cordell, Katia Backho, SOS International, the Gaya police thanna, Gaya Medical College, Joel Guyton Lee, Dan MacNamara, Carolyn Fath, Craig Kilgore, and D. W. Gibson.

Thank you to all my sources. Throughout this book I have changed many names at the request of people who would only speak on the condition of anonymity, or those for whom revealing their identity could be dangerous.

My mother and father, Linda and Wilfred Carney; my sisters, Laura and Allison; my stepmother, Joan Moriarty Carney; and my in-laws, Indira and Govi, have borne the brunt of my odd working schedule, worried as I traveled out on dangerous assignments, and read clumsy early drafts of the manuscript.

Most important, my wife, Padma Govindan, has been a steadfast companion through the darkest hours and the most inspiring moments. She has been a sounding board for all my ideas and a guide on complex issues. I am blessed to have her in my life.

BIBLIOGRAPHY

Anagnost, Ann S. "Strange Circulations: The Blood Economy in Rural China," *Economy and Society* 35, no. 4 (November 2006): 509–29.

Caplan, Arthur. "Transplantation at Any Price?" *American Journal of Transplantation* 4, no. 12 (2004): 1933–34.

Carney, Scott. "My Stint as a Lab Rat," *Isthmus,* December 12, 2005.

———. "Testing Drugs on India's Poor," *Wired News,* December 19, 2005.

Cheney, Anne. *Body Brokers: Inside America's Underground Trade in Human Remains* (New York: Broadway Books, 2006).

Cohen, Lawrence. "Where It Hurts: Indian Material for an Ethics of Organ Transplantation," *Dædalus* 128, no. 4 (1999): 135–65.

Cooper, Melinda. "Experimental Labour—Offshoring Clinical

Trials to China," *East Asian Science, Technology and Society* 2, no. 1 (2008): 73–92.

Elliott, Carl. *Black Hat, White Coat: Adventures on the Dark Side of Medicine* (Boston: Beacon, 2010).

Ernst & Young. *Progressions 2006: Capturing Global Advantage in the Pharmaceutical Industry* (New York: Ernst and Young Global Pharmaceutical Care, 2006).

Fineman, Mark. "Living Off the Dead Is a Dying Trade in Calcutta," *Los Angeles Times,* February 19, 1991.

———. "A Serene, Spiritual Mecca Has Become a Nation of Assassins," *Chicago Tribune,* September 27, 1985.

Goyal, Madhav, Ravindra L. Mehta, Lawrence J. Schneiderman, and Ashwini R. Sehgal. "Economic and Health Consequences of Selling a Kidney in India," *JAMA: The Journal of the American Medical Association* 288, no. 13 (2002): 1589–93.

Ishiguro, Kazuo. *Never Let Me Go* (New York: Knopf, 2005).

Khullar, Mridu. "Americans Seek Stem Cell Treatments in India," *Global Post,* October 6, 2009.

Matas, David, and David Kilgour. *Bloody Harvest: Revised Report into Allegations of Organ Harvesting of Falun Gong Practitioners in China* (2007). http://www. organharvestinvestigation.net.

Milliman Research Report. *2008 U.S. Organ and Tissue Transplant Cost Estimates and Discussion* (Brookfield, WI, 2008).

Petryna, Adriana. "Ethical Variability: Drug Development and Globalizing Clinical Trials," *American Ethnologist* 32, no. 2 (2005): 183–97.

Richardson, Ruth. *Death Dissection and the Destitute* (Chicago: Chicago University Press, 2000).

Roach, Mary. *Stiff: The Curious Lives of Human Cadavers* (New York: Norton, 2004).

Sappol, Michael. "The Odd Case of Charles Knowlton: Anatomical Performance, Medical Narrative, and Identity in Antebellum America," *Bulletin of the History of Medicine* 83, no. 3 (2009): 460–98.

———. *A Traffic in Dead Bodies* (Princeton, NJ: Princeton University Press, 2002).

Scheper-Hughes, Nancy. "The Global Traffic in Human Organs," *Current Anthropology* 41, no. 2 (2000): 191–224.

Sharp, Leslie. *Strange Harvest* (Berkeley: University of California Press, 2006).

Titmuss, Richard. *The Gift Relationship* (London: George Allen & Unwin Ltd., 1970).

Virtue, John. *Leonard and Reva Brooks: Artists in Exile in San Miguel de Allende* (Quebec, Canada: McGill-Queen's University Press, 2001).

Waldby, Catherine, and Robert Mitchell. *Tissue Economies: Blood, Organs, and Cell Lines in Late Capitalism* (Durham, NC: Duke University Press, 2006).

Wang, Guoqi. "Habeus Corpus," *Harpers Magazine,* February 2002.

Weiner, Jonathan. *Long for This World: The Strange Science of Immortality* (New York: Ecco, 2010).

INDEX

Aadil Hospital, 78–79
adoptions, 91–108
  from abstraction to real child, 4
  altruism and, 236
  Banu's case, 100–101
  fees, 94, 96, 97–98, 102, 236
  Hague Convention on, 97–98, 105
  paperwork for, 93–94, 102, 104, 149*n*
  primary criterion in, 7–8
  problems with, 95–98, 102–3
  profit motive in, 97, 103
  Subash's case, 91–94, 98–100, 104–8
Africa, bone factories, 53–54
African-American women, and remy
    hair, 223, 228–29
AIDS. *See* HIV/AIDS
Akanksha Infertility Clinic, *134,*
    135–41, 144–45, 147–48
altruism, 5, 17, 205, 234, 235–36
  blood exchanges and, 10–11, 161, 165

clinical trial subjects and, 179, 181
egg harvesting and, 115, 125–26
hair harvesting and, 225–26
surrogacy and, 146, 150
American Diabetes Association, 211
American Medical Association
    (AMA), 169
American Society of Reproductive
    Medicine, 113–14, 147
Anagnost, Ann S., 192
anatomical skeletons, xiv–xv, 43–44,
    49–50, 52
Anatomy Act of 1832, 49
anonymity, 13–14, 15, 73–75, 80
antibiotics, 200, 201–2, 214
antirejection drugs, 65, 76, 204
Antony, Jeejo, 160–62
Apollo Hospital, 71
Arkansas blood banks, 169–70
Aron, Lavi, 131–32, 133

Aron, Vinesh, 55–56
Avasia, Sunil, 143–44

Baba Raghav Das Hospital, 163–64
Banda, David, 96
Bayer Pharmaceuticals, 176
Ben-Raphael, Zion, 127
Bhasin, J., 103
Bhattacharjee, Bimalendu, 50
Biocon, 189
biosentimentality, 75
Biswas, Mukti, 42–44, 55, 58
black markets, 5, 81–82, 205, 233–34
blood business, 8–11, 153–73, 235
    in China, 192–93
    history of, 8–9, 166–70
    Titmuss and, 9–10, 11, 13, 164–65,
        167–68
    voluntary vs. paid donations, 9–11,
        160–62, 165, 166–70
blood farms, 153–66
    Gorakhpur scandal, 153–64, 170–73
blood plasma, 11, 166–67
Bloody Harvest (Matas and Kilgour), 82–84
Bodh Gaya, 16, 21–36
bodies. *See* human bodies
body snatching, 46–49
Bolivia, 17–18
bone factories, *38,* 39–45, 49–52, 54–58
    author's visit to, xi–xvi, 39–40,
        41–45, 56
    export ban (1985), 40–41, 44n, 52, 55
    history of skeleton trade, 45–52
    production process, 42–44
Box, Mohammed Mullah, 45, 232
Brown, Kimberly, 57
Brown, Tiffany, 229
Buddha (Buddhism), xv, 22
Burke, William, 49
Bush, George W., 197–98

cadaver donation system, 12, 67, 74–75
Calcutta Medical College, 43, 49–50
capitalism. *See* economic issues; profit
    motive
Caplan, Arthur, 81
Cattacha, Vamal, 210–12
Central Bureau of Investigation
    (CBI), 99
cesarean sections (C-sections), 140, 147
Chad, adoption scandals, 96
Chen, Hua, 85–86
Chennai High Court, 99, 101, 108
Cherian, George, 226–27
Chicago Tribune, 50
child development, and orphanages, 8
Children's Home Society & Family
    Services, 103–4
children's skeletons, 51–52
China, 82–89, 96, 188, 192–94
China International Transplantation
    Network Assistance, 84
Cirus, 191
clinical labor, 179
clinical trial lifestyle, 179–80, 180n
clinical trials, 175–95
    approval process, 184, 186
    in China, 188, 192–94
    compensation, 175–76, 179–80
    double standard in, 194–95
    in India, 188–92
    Levitra trial, 175–78, 182–86
    recruitment for, 181–82, 187–88
    safety issues, 176, 177, 184–85
Cohen, Ester, 144–45, 151
Cohen, Lawrence, 7n
commodification of bodies, 4, 14,
    205–6
compensation vs. payment, 114–15,
    122–23, 125–26
consent. *See* informed consent

contract research organizations (CROs), 187–88
Cooper, Melinda, 179, 193–94
Covance, 175–76, 187
Crowe, Sarah, 97
cyclopamine, 190–91
cyclopia, 190–91, 190*n*
Cyprus fertility clinics, 111–12, 114, 116–26

Dalai Lama, 16
da Vinci, Leonardo, 45
death shrouds, 44
de Grey, Aubrey, 200–201
Delhi-IVF, 148–50
Dentsply Rinn, 57
Devaki Hospital, 69, 70
Devi, Gurya, 164, 170
Dexeus, 130
Diflo, Thomas, 87–88
Dom caste, 43, 49–50
"donate," use of term, 5
donor anonymity, 13–14, 15, 73–75, 80
Donor Conception Network, 129
drug trials. *See* clinical trials
Durkin, Therese, 102

economic issues, 205, 234–36
blood donations and, 9–11, 165, 166–70
body parts vs. transplant services, 11–12
clinical trials and, 175–76, 179–80
egg harvesting and, 114–15, 122–23, 125–26
hair trade and, 225–26
international adoptions and, 96, 97–98, 236
kidney donations and, 12, 66–68, 78–81

monetary value of human body, 1–2, 5–6
surrogacy and, 138, 141, 146, 148
egg harvesting, 111–33
altruism and, 115, 125–26
compensation vs. payment, 114–15, 122–23, 125–26
Cyprus fertility clinics, 111–12, 116–26
ethical issues, 113, 115, 125–26
global demand for eggs, 112–13
legal issues, 114–15, 117, 125–26
Russian donors, 119–20, 122, 123–24
in Spain, 127–31
Eisenhower, Dwight D., 166
Elite IVF, 131–33
Elliott, Carl, 180*n*
embryonic stem cell research, 197–200, 213–15
Emily's body, 21–36, *37*
erectile dysfunction trial, 175–78, 182–86
Escuela Universitaria de Bellas Artes, 231–32
Ethica, 146
ethical issues
egg harvesting, 113, 115, 125–26
kidney prospecting, 73–75
surrogacy, 144, 145–46, 150
European Society of Human Reproduction and Embryology (ESHRE), 114–15, 122
European Union (EU), 116–17, 122
exploitation, 10, 14, 80, 88–89, 97, 124, 146, 192–93

Falun Gong, 82–83, 85–87
Families Thru International Adoption, 102
Fatima Hospital, 160–61

Federal Bureau of Investigation (FBI), 106–7
Federal Trade Commission (FTC), 168–69
Fleming, Alexander, 200
Focus on Children, 96
Food and Drug Administration (FDA), 177, 185, 189, 194, 202
funeral parlors, thefts of bodies, 17

Ganla, Kedar, 148–49
Gaya Medical College, 23, 25–26, 30–32
Gelsinger, Jesse, 176–77
Genentech, 191, 207–8
gene therapy, 176–77, 202
Gift Relationship, The (Titmuss), 9–10, 11, 13, 14–15, 164–65
Gillette, 12
Gorakhpur blood farms, 153–64, 170–73
Gore, Al, 11
grave robberies (grave robbers), xii, xiv, 42, 45–49, 51–52, 232–33
gray markets, 5, 117
Gupta, Anoop, 142, 148–50
Gupta, K. K., 226
Gupta Enterprises, 226
Gurtner, Geoffrey, 212
Guzman, Juan, 231–32
Gwong Detention Center, 86–87

Hague Convention on Intercountry Adoption, 97–98, 105
hair harvesting, *220,* 221–29
Haiti, adoption scandals, 96
Hardesty, Loretta, *230,* 231–32, 238
Hare, William, 48–49
Harvard Medical School, 53
Hassina, Alma, 133

heart transplants, 11–12
hemoglobin, 155
Henan drug trial, 192–94
hepatitis, 10, 165, 168, 170
Hiranandani Hospital, 142, 148–49
HIV/AIDS, 162–63, 165, 169, 193–94, 202
Hoksbergen, René, 105
human bodies
    as commodities, 4, 14, 205–6
    man vs. meat, 1–19
    monetary value of, 1–2, 5–6
    story of Emily's body, 21–36
human bone factories. *See* bone factories
human cloning, 206–7
human egg harvesting. *See* egg harvesting
human growth hormone (HGH), 207–8
human kidneys. *See* kidney prospecting
human life span, 200
Human Studies Review Board (HSRB), 189
hydrochloric acid, 42, 43
hyperstimulation syndrome (HSS), 126

iChild, 102–3
India
    adoption scandals. *See* adoptions
    author's start in, 15–17
    blood farms. *See* blood farms
    bone factories. *See* bone factories
    clinical trials, 188–92
    egg harvesting, 116–17
    Emily's death and body, 21–23
    hair harvesting, 221–29
    human remains export ban (1985), 40–41, 44*n,* 52, 55

kidney prospecting. *See* kidney
  prospecting
surrogacy tourism. *See* surrogacy
  tourism
Indian Council of Medical Research
  (ICMR), 142, 147
Indian Drug Control General, 189
Indian Ocean tsunami (2004), 61–62
IndUShealth, 67
informed consent, 11, 40, 58, 189,
  193–94
inmates. *See* prisoners
Institut Marquès, *110,* 127–29
Internal Revenue Service (IRS), 179
international adoptions. *See* adoptions
International IVF&PGD Centre,
  117–21
International Organization for Stan-
  dardization (ISO), 78–79
Iran, 81–82, 89
Ishiguro, Kazuo, 207
Israel, 18, 113, 127
Iswarya Fertility Centre, 142–43
Ivanovina, Galina, 119–21
IVF (in vitro fertilization), 111–13, 114,
  117, 125, 127–28

Jayakumar, Ramani, 101
Jindal, Seema, 149–50
Jordan, Kristen, 139, 141, 148–49

Kansas blood banks, 168–69
Karkhanis, Amit, 146, 148
Karppiah, K., 73
Kasturba Gandhi Hospital, 191
Kennedy, Samuel, 53
Khan, Javed Ahmed, 54–55
Khullar, Mridu, 214
kidney prospecting, 17, 61–89
  in China, 82–89

economic issues, 12, 66–68,
  78–81, 84
impression of scarcity and, 76–79
privacy ethic and, 73–75
social side effects of selling kidneys,
  6–7, *7n*
transplant lists, 12, 66–67, 76–79, 89
Tsunami Nagar refugee camp,
  61–65, 68–74
kidney waiting lists, 12, 66–67, 76–79
Kilgore, Charles, 53, 54
Kilgore, Craig, 50, 53–54
Kilgore International, 50, 53–54
Kilgour, David, 82–84, 88
Knowlton, Charles, 46–47
Koundouros, Savvas, 120–21, 125–26,
  197–98, 206, 219
Kumar, Rajeev, 58

Laksh Hotel, 144–45
Landsteiner, Karl, 8–9
Laogai Research Foundation, 83
L-cystine, 224
Letrozole, 189–91
Levitra trial, 175–78, 182–86
Life (magazine), *230,* 232
Liston, Robert, 203
Long for this World (de Grey), 200–201

McCulloch, Ernest Armstrong, 199
McGee, Glenn, 117, 122, 133
Madonna, 96
Mahabharata, 223
Malaysian Social Services (MSS), *90,*
  93–96, 98–100, 104
Mandal, Rubina, 140–41
Manoharan, G. P., 93–94
man vs. meat, 1–19
Matas, David, 82–84
medical grafts, 40, 201

medical schools, and grave robberies, 45–47, 52–53
Meir, Yehonnatan, 133
miracle cures, 199–201
money issues. *See* economic issues
Montuschi, Olivia, 129
Mother Jones, 16, 100, 107
Murphy, Keith, 215–18
Muthuvel, Arun, 143

Nath, Kedar, 171–73
National Organ Transplant Act, 11, 78
Nepal, 138, 170
Never Let Me Go (Ishiguro), 207
9/11 terrorist attacks (2001), 167*n*
Northwick Park Hospital, 176

Obama, Barack, 198
Oliveras, Joseph, 128–29
Oprah (TV show), 135–36, 145
Organovo, *196,* 215–18
organ printing, *196,* 216–17
organ prospecting. *See* kidney prospecting
organ scarcity, 76–79
organ transplant lists, 11–13, 66–67, 76–79, 89
Osta International, 57–58
ovarian hyperstimulation syndrome (OHSS), 126

Pagari, Chaya, 148
paid donations, 67, 76–77, 80–82, 164–70
Pal, Manoj, 42–43
Pandey, Chakrapani, 171–73
Parikh, O. P., 162–63
Patel, Nayna, 135–36, 139, 141–42, 144–45, 147–50
Pauquette Adoption Services, 101–4

penicillin, 200
Peterson, Beth, 102–3
Petra Clinic, 118–21, 125
Petryna, Adriana, 181–82
Pfizer, 176
pharmaceutical trials. *See* clinical trials
phases of clinical trials, 184
Philippine Information Agency, 79
Philpott, Sean, 188–89
Pilgrim, David, 103–4
Pislaru, Carmen, 124
pituitary glands, 17, 208
Prasad, Srirupa, 192
Preet Mandir, 103–4
Premier Research Group, 187
prisoners
    anatomical skeletons, 49–50
    blood donations, 10, 169–70
    Chinese kidney harvesting, 82–89
    drug trials, 181, 186
privacy issues, 13–14, 15, 17, 73–75, 234. *See also* donor anonymity
professional guinea pigs. *See* clinical trials
profit motive, 11–12
    in blood donations, 166–70
    in clinical trials, 179–80
    in internal organ sales, 75, 78, 80, 88–89
    in international adoptions, 97, 103
    in surrogacy, 141, 146, 149–50
Prozac, 202

Rabo India Finance, 188
racial issues, 7–8, 129–30
Raghupati, K., 101
Raj Impex, 226–28
Ramachandran, K. K. S. R., 64–65
Rana, Sanju, 150
Rao, Nageshwar, 93, 98–100, 105–8, *109*

Ravindranath, Dinesh, 95
Red Cross, 166
Reddy, K. C., 80–81
red markets, overview, 5–7
regenerative medicine, 197–219
Reknas Company, 50–51
remy hair, 223–24, 227–29
replacement body parts, 215–18
Reproductive Genetics Institute, 118–19
research subjects. *See* clinical trials
Rodriguez, Nicole, 129
Ruediger, Christian, 57

Samoa, adoption scandals, 96
San Miguel de Allende, Mexico, 231–32
Sappol, Michael, 46, 47*n*, 49
Sarkar, Jayant, 156–57
scarcity, and organ-harvesting network, 76–79
Scheper-Hughes, Nancy, 75–77, 81–82
Selvam, Maria, 61–65
sex selection, 117, 132–13
Shankar, S., 98, 99, 106–7
Shantha Biotech, 189
Sharp, Leslie, 74–75
Shatzky, Omer, 131–32, 133
Sheikh, Abdul Waheed, 79
Sher, David, 131–33
Shroff, Geeta, 213–15
shrunken heads, 18
Singer, Peter, 124
Singh, K. M., 163
Sisti, Claudia, 130
Sitla Hospital, *152,* 171–72
Sivagama, 92–94, 98–100, 104–8, *109*
skeleton trade. *See* bone factories
Smerdon, Usha, 146
Smolin, David, 97–98

social classes, and red markets, 6–7
soul, 3, *3n*
Spain, egg harvesting, 127–31
Sri Tirumula Temple, 221–26
Srivastav, Vishwajeet, 156
Stanford Medical School, 52
stem cell research, 197–200, 209–19
Strange Harvest (Sharp), 74–75
Subash, 92–94, 98–100, 104–8, *109*
Subrammaniyan, S. R., 210–12
Sujiatun Hospital, 82–83
Sun Pharmaceuticals, 189
supply and demand, 12–13, 81–82, 205, 234–35
surgical innovation, 202–3
surrender deeds, 93–94, 95, 97, 102, 104
surrogacy tourism, 135–51
    Akanksha clinic, 135–41, 144–45, 147–48
    contracts, 138, 141, 144, 146, 147
    costs and surrogate payments, 138, 141, 146, 148
    ethical issues, 144, 145–46, 150
    explosion in India, 141–42
    regulatory issues, 142–44, 146–47
synthetic market, 206–9, 218

tea stalls, 71*n,* 72
TGN1412, 176
thalassemia, 121
Till, James, 199
Titmuss, Richard, 9–10, 11, 13, 14–15, 164–65, 167–68
Toole, Lynn, 101–2
Traffic in Dead Bodies, A (Sappol), 46, 49
transparency, 14, 18–19, 80, 89, 236–38
transplant lists, 11–13, 66–67, 76–79, 89
Trokoudes, Krinos, 111–12, *116,* 116–18, 122, 206

Tsunami Nagar refugee camp, 61–65, 68–74
Tuskegee syphilis studies, 181

UNICEF, 97
United Group Programs, 67
United Network for Organ Sharing (UNOS), 12, 76
University of Wisconsin-Madison, 16, 175

Varanasi, 16, 23
Vassiliou, Androulla, 122
Verlinsky, Oleg, 118–21
Verlinsky, Yuri, 118
Viagra trial, 175–78, 182–86
Vioxx, 202
Viral Genetics, 193–94
vitamin E, 182
voluntary blood donations, 9–11, 160–62, 165, 166–70

Waldby, Catherine, 179, 204
Wang, Guoqi, 83–84, 88
Weiner, Jonathan, 200
White Coat, Black Hat (Elliott), 180*n*
white markets, 5
Winfrey, Oprah, 135–36, 145
Wired News, 16, 190–91, 212
Wisconsin Department of Children and Families, 102
World Health Organization (WHO), 79–80, 233–34
World War II, 9–10, 166–67
Wu, Harry, 83

Yadhav, Papu, 154–57, 159–62, 170
Young Brothers, 43–44, 54–56, *59*

Zavos, Panayiotis Michael, 206
Zoe's Ark, 96